TEARING DOWN THE WALL

THE CONTEMPORARY GUIDE TO DECODING

PINK FLOYD THE WALL

ONE BRICK AT A TIME

MARK YOSHIMOTO NEMCOFF

WORDSUSHI BOOKS

A DIVISION OF GLENNEYRE PRESS

LOS ANGELES, CA

ISBN: 1-934602-27-2
ISBN-13: 978-1-934602-27-0

Published by
Glenneyre Press, LLC.
Los Angeles, CA
www.wordsushi.com

First Edition

Cover design by: MYN

A NOTE FROM THE AUTHOR

This analysis is solely about the double album *The Wall* by Pink Floyd. It is neither about the movie nor the most recent tour. No disrespect intended to Alan Parker's vision and interpretation, but due to the limitations of storytelling on film, you do yourself and this brilliant work a disservice if you believe the movie adaptation is the definitive version. There is so much more here — some of which may astound you.

Let me be clear: this is *my* interpretation of *The Wall*. You may hear things completely differently; as they say, "your mileage may vary." What you hear and feel in this music is an extension of your individuality and who you are, all colored by the combined experiences you've had in life.

Think of this as an extended commentary, like you would find on a DVD or Blu-Ray. For maximum effect, loop each individual track of *The Wall* as you read about the amazing elements hidden within these songs.

A CONTEMPORARY GUIDE TO

PART ONE

DECODING PINK FLOYD - THE WALL

PART TWO

WORDS ARE, OF COURSE, THE MOST POWERFUL DRUG USED BY MANKIND.

- Rudyard Kipling

PART ONE

IN THE FLESH .?

This is where it all begins, amidst the fire and song, the wire and the wood.

We smash cut to an explosion on a darkened stage, entering this world kicking and screaming. Pyrotechnics fly as the opening salvo of music is catapulted directly upon the faithful and adoring. The band's thunderous intro is so fierce, as it pounds those opening chords through thousands of amplified watts of sonic power, that it grabs thousands of fans by the throat with an unbreakable grip. The great, throbbing throng, all looking for something to *feel*, pushes closer to the stage to get something they can never have: a true glimpse at the man.

Why? Behind those eyes, Pink is very much a man sheltering a scared and wounded child within. Tonight, a truly dark night of the soul, will be a journey of self-discovery.

It will not be an easy passage.

In fact, Pink will experience torment enough to strip away his very soul. Will he be strong enough to get it back?

The clues to this rich, deep psychological puzzle begin seventeen seconds earlier, somewhere outside as the sun shines on a field the color of dark summer jade. From afar, they come — a small group of buskers, musical vagabonds really, playing their instruments as if they can summon a spirit from beyond an enormous wall that reaches unnaturally into the sky. Their tune is a pastoral incantation, challenging the unalienable forces of nature to allow them to take their comrade home.

The first seventeen seconds of *The Wall* are themselves a small puzzle piece. What I came to realize as I closely examined this sonically rich album and all of the gems, clues and Easter eggs hidden inside, was there was zero chance this intro of sorts did not have a viable significance of its own.

The tune, evocative of music from a different era, is in fact a continuation of "Outside the Wall," the track which closes the final half of this deep narrative. Here, it begins with an abrupt and cryptic spoken sound bite: "We came in…"

These words, the very first uttered by Roger Waters on the album, sound like the tail end of a fractured sentence, the full meaning of which we are not allowed to grasp. Buried low in the mix, they almost seem like the by-product of some impromptu conversation barely caught on mic while the tape was rolling. However, I must question if that could be the case or that the exact wording is unintentional — because one of the things that becomes quite apparent listening to *The Wall* is that *nothing* appears in the mix by accident. Every little sound advances the story.

This pastoral tune has a decidedly Word War II era musical sensibility; the melody is carried by a clarinet, an instrument that is all but obsolete in modern music but was extremely prevalent in the type of swing that became popular in dance halls, table top radios and record players of the time. There is significance; World War II plays a large part in this allegorical tale of isolation and madness, which will become evident later in the album.

Finally, the big rock and roll salvo erupts, a grand spectacle, one that mirrors the grand spectacle of birth itself: you enter the world, the stage of life, screaming your lungs out as others watch your every move. Let's not forget that birth is also the first event of our lives that is not of our own personal choosing.

Musically speaking, the band makes a very interesting choice here: the intro, with those acoustic minstral strains of "Outside the Wall," is in the key of B major. If you aren't musically inclined, don't worry, I'll simplify for you. Songs in major keys tend to be about happy and positive things while those in minor keys, obviously, sound a bit sadder and moodier. Here, you could categorize the melody played by the clarinet as "hopeful." This is very much set up by the interval jump taken by the first two notes.

That interval, the distance between the first note and the second in terms of its musical scale, is a perfect 4th. Before I stray too far from my musical over-simplification, the "perfect 4th" is a very keystone interval jump used in harmony. Moreover, it's a very *recognizable* two-note interval jump. Close your eyes and think of the first two notes in "Here Comes the Bride" or "We Wish You a Merry Christmas." You'll hear that same perfect 4th interval.

The reason I'm placing this seemingly innocuous two-note interval under the microscope is because this is an example of a common practice in music and film scoring: using certain sounds and melodic intervals to cue your subconscious mind into understanding what amounts to a sort of pop-cultural emotional shorthand. Music, a true global language, can speak in the abstract to paint a visual picture in your mind. You don't need lyrics to understand the triumphant evocation of the main title theme from *Star Wars*, nor would you mistake the sound of Darth Vader's "Imperial March" for anything other than menacing and foreboding.

One of the things that makes *The Wall* so fascinating is a very pervasive use of musical elements — interesting sonic nuggets buried in the mix to vividly fill in the story. As you begin to hone in on them, you'll note how they not only relate to the underlying subconscious narrative elements of Pink's life and the emotional turmoil he's going through, but also use abstraction to enhance specific things occurring in the background without pulling you out of the story.

Structurally-speaking, *The Wall* very much follows a cinematic three-act structure common to film. The very beginning of the first act introduces the protagonist in his natural element. *The Wall* is no different, as we go from that hopeful B major key into a darker E minor during "In the Flesh?" — a sonic portrayal of a normal moment in Pink's life. As he is a rock star, that moment naturally occurs on stage during a concert.

As the band kicks in to the very uniform opening of this rock opera, it implies a rhythmic quality akin to a grand march. We hear a parallel with the first auditory salvo simulating the explosive opening of a rock show: bombastic drums playing with almost militaristic precision. The sound of the Hammond organ — its long chords and place in the mix resembling the wailing of human voices – carries a gospel quality, adding to the pseudo-religious vibe. The blaring rock-n-roll pomp-and-circumstance quantized to the nature of the beat implies *spectacle*.

Here we discover Waters setting up musical motifs in the same way master film music composer John Williams uses *leitmotif* — signature musical themes for different characters such as the aforementioned "Imperial March." These motifs are later revisited within the structure and arrangement of other songs in *The Wall*, bringing us back to the emotional beats Waters has already taught us to feel.

See? Emotional shorthand.

Once Pink begins singing in this triplet rhythm, the kick (bass) drum plays a pattern reminiscent of a heartbeat, very similar to the heartbeat that opens and closes *Dark Side of the Moon*. This internal rhythm is a perfect match to the lyrics – literally Pink's own, subconscious thoughts. Whether he is actually singing them to his audience via his in-concert alter ego is less important overall than the realization that these are his true feelings and, without a doubt, demonstrate an obvious level of discontent about his life.

He tells them that they have no idea who he is, that they will never see behind the mask he hides behind. When he sings about them having to claw their way through this disguise, he means he will not give up his true self without a fight. He is very protective and distances himself from those who seek to know him. Perhaps even himself?

Here you are as a rock star, but you're not happy because you aren't really you.

It was the best of times. It was the worst of times, indeed.

Keep note of this twisted mirror image dichotomy; as we continue through the narrative of *The Wall*, you'll see how this Yin/Yang motif continues to play a significant psychological measure in Pink's life.

The harmonic voices of the background singers bring a somewhat wholesome sound to the mix, imbuing the piece with a completely subversive counterpoint. Listen to the thick, strong major chord harmonies: there's an element of Beach Boys and a bit of 50's do-wop. Take away the vocals and you'd probably think it was a happy song. That is why I believe these lyrics live only in Pink's subconscious rather than being part of the song he's performing. He's only delivering this venomous invective to the audience on the inside, where all of his troubles are brewing.

Production-wise, the slapback echo on Pink's voice is not only symbolic of the large hall in which he performs, but also of the repetition of this forced performance, night after night, an unsatisfying repetition, ad nauseum, when the passion for this audience is gone.

Consider, for a moment, the lyric "Space cadet glow…" Here you have the beaming faces of the stoned or of the *"sheeple"* in the audience, whose own lack of intelligence makes them the prime followers of any cult of personality. These are people who need to be told what to do, how to think, how to act — whose very allegiance gives them a sense of meaning and purpose in lives that would otherwise be full of fear and uncertainty. They are empty vessels, often lied to and taken advantage of for the purpose of fulfilling someone else's agenda.

In an interesting use of foreshadowing, "In The Flesh?" gives us a very deep, brilliant first look into the character of Pink and illuminates the cracks in his foundation (without revealing too much!) that will require him to change as all good protagonists must. Before we know it, we're at the crescendo of this "performance;" the low end mechanical rumbling begins, and you can almost sense these sheeple being steamrolled by some giant machine. They are just grist for some massive mill. After all, man reduced to faceless fodder is a theme that recurs throughout *The Wall*.

This mechanical rumbling evolves into the rising propeller pitch of a dive-bomber closing in on its target. We follow a synthetic whistle of its falling ordinance, but instead of an explosion we are greeted with the sound of a wailing baby.

From the war machine's cry of death comes the cry of life anew.

Because this is where…"We came in…" This is where it all begins, entering this world kicking and screaming.

※ ※ ※ ※ ※

BRICK BY BRICK
(A DELAYED INTRODUCTION)

Take red, the color of blood, and white, the color of innocence, mix them together on a palate and you get pink.

Art — because it generates wonder and achievement and sometimes demands us to ask questions about ourselves — stands as pure evidence that we, as humans, exist. An artist's responsibility therefore is to embody this in his work, no matter the medium. Whether the canvas is composed of stretched linen and paint or music and lyrics doesn't matter; the only requirement is that creation somehow captures an essential truth, an irretrievable moment in time, or an undeniable emotion.

The Wall, originally released in November of 1979, is a remarkable and thematically-rich canvas made powerful not only by how deeply it draws upon some very essential human struggles, but also the crafty way it ultimately reveals itself as a philosophical treatise about our interpersonal relationships. Seen by some as a story merely about how someone disintegrates when they become isolated, or how we, as a society, disintegrate when isolated from one another, Roger Waters' semi-autobiographical rock opera about a burned-out rock star suffering a dark night of the soul while trying to examine his unhappiness — and along the way is haunted by his unhappy memories of his domineering mother, abusive schoolteacher and distant wife — is a deliberate gape down dark, uncomfortable corridors of the soul, searching for that wounded child within; a work that uses complex narrative structures to express typical Modernist concerns such as the shattering of consciousness and the decay of modern society. Brilliantly crafted into the album's message and production are elements of a philosophy about the meaning of human existence that tread on the mental real estate owned by giants like Freud, Sartre, Camus, Kafka, Orwell and Kubrick, among others. Some of these tiny, bare glimpses into existentialism are so brilliantly woven into the framework of *The Wall* that they remain mostly subliminal; yet there are few who listen to this work that don't feel it somehow resonate within them.

To think it all began with a moment of temporary insanity and gob of spit.

Dark Side of the Moon had come out in March of 1973. Although the album was about the isolation of insanity, it was not about Syd Barrett, the former Floyd frontman whose own mental demons, exacerbated by drug use, led to his ouster from the band half a decade earlier. Nonetheless, the ghost of Syd's presence was still thematically evident in their work. Originally *Dark Side of the Moon* had a secondary title: *A Piece for Assorted Lunatics.*

By the summer of 1977, after two more albums, *Wish You Were Here* and *Animals,* Pink Floyd found itself on tour once again. The truth was the band didn't want to do it anymore. The success of *Dark Side of the Moon* had catapulted Pink Floyd into the mainstream pop culture consciousness. The band finally felt they had reached all of the goals they had dreamed of achieving musically. Although the impact on them as artists was unclear at the time, the relationships between the four band members began to deteriorate as a result.

They were all on different wavelengths now, even though they had known each other for quite a long time. Roger Waters had met other original Floyd members Richard Wright and Nick Mason at the Regent Street Polytechnic School of Architecture where he studied Mechanical Engineering.

To make things worse, Waters had begun to feel that the audience was no longer listening. He was frustrated spending so much time and effort crafting music and lyrics yet the first six rows were shouting and yelling throughout the whole show as if they were cheering on a football game. To Waters, these weren't people who bought a concert ticket for the music; these were people who paid for the party and the spectacle, an audience half-full of assholes screaming all the time.

During the tour, Waters' behavior toward the concert crowds became increasingly aggressive and abusive. It would be during the tour's final show, on July 6 at Olympic Stadium in Montreal, that things went beyond the point of no return. Waters attempted to play the beginning of "Pigs on the Wing (Part 2)" only to be interrupted by the loud pop of firecrackers near the stage. He restarted the song, only to be interrupted again — not just once, but three more times. Upon the fourth restart, after managing to get past the first line, *another* loud crack split the air.

Waters lost it. "Oh... for fuck's sake, stop letting off fireworks and shouting and screaming, I'm trying to sing a song! I mean I don't care, if you don't want to hear it, you know... fuck you. I'm sure there are a lot of people here who do want to hear it. Why don't you just be quiet? You want to let your fireworks off go outside and let them off out there. And if you want to shout and scream and holler go do it out there, but I'm trying to sing a song that some people want to listen to it. I want to listen to it."

A short while later, when one of the crazed teenage fans in the front row tried climbing onto the stage, Waters became unhinged and spat in the unruly kid's face.

He would immediately regret that momentary lapse of judgment. The rest of the band, already at odds with each other, had now seen everything. David Gilmour declined to participate in the acoustic encore and a small riot at the front of the stage followed the band's eventual exit.

The next day, realizing he had been reduced to something almost inhuman, albeit just for a mere moment, Waters had an epiphany that involved the theatrical idea of building a wall across the front of the stage to express his long-brewing sense of alienation and separation between himself and the audience.

Pink Floyd by this time was a hugely successful rock band like Led Zeppelin or Deep Purple. There was, however, a huge, defining difference: the members of Pink Floyd were not *individual* stars. Perhaps this reason drove Roger Waters to eschew the band's normal collaborative process and begin demoing this new concept on his own. Whatever the reason, Waters mind bloomed. During a meeting with the band and their management, Waters played them the seminal ideas behind both *The Wall* and the album that would one day become his solo record, *The Pros and Cons of Hitchhiking*. (It should be historically noted that only the management voted for *Hitchhiking* as Pink Floyd's next album; though, in their defense, at that time the demos did not include such definitive songs such as "Comfortably Numb" or "Run like Hell.")

Intended to be a multimedia experience from the beginning, especially with the inclusion of biting graphic artwork by Gerald Scarfe, one of the leading political cartoonists of the modern age, the band immediately recognized *The Wall* had the potential to become an important work, not only as a daring form of social theatre, but from a philosophical point of view as well. There were obvious larger differences brewing in this evolution of the band and the depth of their message, and *The Wall* spoke to that. Whereas *Dark Side of the Moon* was an album about the isolation of insanity, *The Wall* was rooted in how insanity alienates people from the rest of the world.

Ultimately, the decision to embark on another album was driven by financial reasons. The band had unfortunately had trusted their money to a financial broker who eventually fled to Spain and was later arrested and sentenced for financial fraud. Bad investments, made without the band's knowledge, left the members of Pink Floyd over £1 million in debt and facing a crushing tax liability of over £12 million. In order to get out from underneath their mounting monetary woes, the band would have to spend a year outside of the U.K.

Though they had been fleshing out *The Wall* at their own Brittania Row Studios in London, recording for the album began in earnest in January of 1979 in a studio named Super Bear, high up in the Alpes-Maratimes, a half hour outside of Nice, France.

Hot for a big holiday release, Dick Asher at Sony/CBS Records told Waters they would increase the band's royalty share if they could deliver a completed album by November. Waters agreed. The band booked a second studio: Mirival, fifty miles away, owned by Jazz pianist Jacques Loussier and built inside a fake chateau where one could dive off the wall and swim in the moat.

The album had begun despite obvious acrimony between band members; what little detente existed began falling apart because of the fast-approaching deadline. When Keyboardist Richard Wright refused to return early from his summer vacation to record his tracks, Waters had had enough. Richard Wright had a fragile confidence; he was shy, silent, and introverted — always apart from the rest of the band. This final insult, coupled with the tension created when Wright asked to be a producer on the album — an idea producer Bob Ezrin was not fond of – caused Waters to demand that founding member Wright be fired from the band. Otherwise, Waters would pull the plug on Pink Floyd.

Waters did stipulate that Wright could stay on as a paid band member for the length of the tour but after that, he was gone. Surprisingly, Wright agreed, possibly tired of fifteen years of band politics and the growing rift and power struggles between Pink Floyd's self-appointed leader Roger Waters and David Gilmour, who was unhappy at the lack of recognition he was receiving for his contribution to *The Wall*.

This great band, which had once shared a democratic methodology in both creative and business affairs, was now turning into a dictatorship. The irony was inescapable. Band members who were suffering from the inability to talk to each other and discuss their problems were now creating great philosophical work about the suffering human beings and human relationships have when there is a lack of communication.

What began as Roger's vision would remain that way until the bitter end. Because of, or perhaps despite Richard Wright's departure, *The Wall* is not as keyboard heavy as previous Pink Floyd albums. In the spaces where synths previously filled in the emotional counterpoint, especially on *Dark Side of the Moon*, instead there is an orchestra led by composer/arranger Michael Kamen, who would later go on to score movies such as *Die Hard* and *Mr. Holland's Opus*. Because of the public's general understanding of the nuance of orchestral score in modern music, it became possible to paint detailed musical mind-pictures that could be easily achieved with a broader stroke, esoteric and abstract musical stylings of the synthesizers of that era.

While there had always been definitive mood evocation in the music of Pink Floyd, *The Wall* holds a tremendous amount of the narrative in the form of the musical arrangements within the songs themselves. Coupled with the imagery-rich audio production of Bob Ezrin, cleverly hidden in the mixes are wonderful examples where instruments not only enhance the imagery of the narrative, but also tell a story within the story — sometimes even invoking an outside reference to one of the many related works that *The Wall* draws from.

Though there are several musical and narrative moments in the album that seem to have been influenced by such literary-driven work as *Lord of the Flies*, *The Shining*, *A Christmas Carol*, *The Old Man and the Sea*, *Johnny Got His Gun*, *A Brave New World*, among many others — and you can point to deeply obvious Freudian themes in the battle between Pink's Id and Ego — *The Wall* is not some sort of mash-up of the pop culture psychology of the time. Waters is no thief. Instead, what he has done is to create a completely original work of art that uses our grounding in these popular message-driven narratives to add incredible depth to the mosaic of understanding of our own internal voices.

Regardless of how you feel about the philosophical aspects of *The Wall*, it is an extraordinary work of art whose social relevance is as powerful now as it was the day it was created. Perhaps it's because certain parallels between *The Wall* and much of our recent history are disturbing. Or maybe it's because every good story is, in some aspect, a retelling of "Faust" — deals are made and the battles for fought for one's soul. Art should stand as a metaphor for something that speaks about the human condition and most importantly the search for the truth. The true artist, through his exaggeration, distortion, reflection and shorthand, sheds light on those simple truths you may not have consciously considered before and lets you see them clearly — if you know where to look.

Or, in the case of *The Wall*, if you know *when* to listen.

*****

THE THIN ICE

The baby's cry segues us directly into "The Thin Ice" as we delve further into Pink's anguish-driven, self-examination of the soul. Symbolically, this is the continuation of life from birth as we visit Pink's infancy.

Examining the first half of *The Wall*, it becomes clear how much of the narrative actually takes place in flashback. What makes this device all the more interesting is that we, the listener, are *not* being transported to those by gone days to see the way things actually used to be. We are not standing over Pink's shoulder as these visions are presented to him. In "The Thin Ice", we effectively *are* Pink, or at the very least a passive passenger inside of Pink's mind. Nearly all of *The Wall's* narrative takes place inside Pink's brain; what you are hearing are not the actual voices of other people in his life, but Pink's remembrance and interpretation of what he feels they said to him. What you are hearing are the ghosts living inside his mind, filtered through his psychosis; these are the voices inside of Pink's consciousness. Despite the serene piano accompanying his thoughts, his consciousness is definitely not happy with what resides there.

Waters subconsciously evokes a sense of nostalgia in the songwriting by utilizing what is known as a 1,6,4,5 chord progression. Unofficially known by musicians as the "oldies" progression, 1,6,4,5 has an identifiably 1950's feel to it; it's the same exact chord progression used in era-defining classic hits such as "Earth Angel" by the Penguins, "Duke of Earl" by Gene Chandler and "Stand By Me" by Ben E. King. Here, Waters takes us sonically back to the music of his own — and by extension, Pink's — early youth.

That's not to say 1,6,4,5 isn't a commonly used chord progression today. You can hear it in modern hits like "No Surprises" by Radiohead or even "Baby" by Justin Bieber. However, compared with modern rock and roll — especially the bombastic rock overture we hear Pink perform during "In the Flesh?" — music from the 1950's has a very innocent quality. We're talking about music from a time before advanced knowledge and technology that we share today. It is no accident that the innocence of this form of rock music is used to parallel Pink's own innocence as an infant.

From this flashback, the voice of Pink's mother — as portrayed by David Gilmour in a somewhat soothing voice carrying a nursery-rhyme-simple melody — first arises. Take notice of the self-referential moniker of "Momma."

A hint as to how far back into Pink's life this examination occurs is the use of present tense: "Daddy loves you, too." Present tense tells us this lullaby is first being sung while Pink's father is still alive, signifying a moment in time before his (and to a similar extent Waters' own) father is killed in battle during World War II,

Here we also have the introduction of what will be a recurring motif where Mother refers to Pink as "babe." This won't be the last time.

We are also introduced to another interesting, recurring theme of this pastoral picture of Pink's past: blue.

There's a clever dichotomy at play with the color blue. Blue is often associated with feelings of calmness and serenity. It's often described as peaceful and orderly, especially the shade of "baby blue." These all parallel the same "oldies" sensibility the background music evokes.

But that's not all. Blue can also be associated with feelings of sadness or aloofness. Which is in use here, you ask: serenity or sadness?

Both.

We are presented with a Yin/Yang; in the twisted mirror, we see the opposite. Ironically, in photographic terms, it would be comparable to a film's *negative*.

We began this song with David Gilmour as the reassuring, benevolent voice of Momma, singing baby a lullaby. When Momma sings, "the sea may look warm to you babe. And the sky make look blue," she's telling us not to be fooled by what things appear to be. This is, of course, an overwhelmingly common lesson for parents to teach and re-teach to their children. However, when Gilmour's Momma says it, she's very much glossing over the issue.

But when we are then presented with Roger Waters as Momma's flashback voice, the lyrics deliver a distinct counterpoint, essentially presenting us with that film negative of these serene snapshots from Pink's infancy.

Before we go further down that road, let's step back a bit. Within the realm of dream analysis, *ice* is associated with subconscious feelings of fear that disaster is about to strike unless something is done to avert it. Dreams involving ice commonly suggest a fear or anxiety about death and/or psychological issues that are negative in nature and are still inaccessible by your conscious self.

Waters' Momma represents more of this subconscious truth. This is not so much her saying *things aren't exactly what they seem,* as much as it is a dire warning.

If you should go skating on the thin ice of modern life.

Dragging behind you the silent reproach of a million tear-stained eyes.

This is very significant, because Momma is talking about the weight one carries from the expectations of those who have come before us, our relatives, and our forefathers. These are truly the sins of the father visited upon the son. What "The Thin Ice" represents, then, is a lament from Pink as to how none of us are really born with a clean slate.

There is also an intentional double meaning at play here. Those "million tear stained eyes" could also belong to Pink's loyal followers; if so, those aren't tears of sorrow, but instead tears of elation from worshipping at the feet of their rock idol.

Remember, it is this pressure, these expectations in Pink's life (and as documented by the spitting incident, in Roger's life as well) that are causing the rupture of Pink's psychological foundation,— the same one Pink has now discovered is constructed of thin ice.

Don't be surprised if a crack in the ice appears under your feet.

You slip out of your depth and out of your mind.

With your fear flowing out behind you as you claw the thin ice.

Again a mention of clawing — this time as a primal survival mechanism. The utilization, though, is brilliantly reversed from "In the Flesh?" where have those rabid fans trying to desperately claw their way through Pink's mask in order to know the "true face" of their idol. Here in "The Thin Ice," however, it is Pink who is trapped below the surface of the water, which once may have seemed warm and blue, and is desperately trying to claw his way out.

Instead, the nightmare image in his mind has him sinking with his fear flowing out behind him; a scream trails from his lungs as he plummets into the frigid darkness to meet a terrible fate.

The essence of the song is the terrible realization of the dirty secret that modern life offers no more than thin ice, a fragile floor upon which to stand. Thematically speaking, however, this song really introduces us to the dynamic of differentiating what people say versus what they really mean.

Herein lays the essence of why this particular event is so important to the narrative. It establishes a certain understanding within Pink's mind, the "a-ha" moment which is essential to any protagonist's growth. As Pink examines these vignettes from his past, these voices are all inside Pink's head. This isn't his actual mother speaking; instead, these characterizations are his mind's representations of her as filtered through his memories and recollections. Later in the first half of *The Wall* we will hear voices of people who enter this narrative — specifically his wife's lover and a groupie — who are the embodiments of those existing outside of Pink's mind that drive the narrative in their own fashion.

I would be hard-pressed to condemn Momma's soft-peddling of the cruel realities of the world as outright lies. However, it is here where Pink's mind journeys, giving the distinct impression that within these *little white lies* is a certain amount of resentment. Being protected from the truth of the modern world has left him unprepared to handle the way the world really treats him.

That warm sea is terribly frigid.

"The Thin Ice" is made up of three distinct sections. The first is Gilmour's Momma. The second part, beginning just over one minute into the song, is the negative.

But the third part, the instrumental section — that's the moment of realization as we mind-travel back into the present from this newly-framed remembrance of the past. Here, another bombastic rock spectacle similar to the opening chords of "In the Flesh?" is used as a *leitmotif* that alludes to the spectacle of the concert and Pink's life on stage; it speaks to the subconscious genesis driving the dark moodiness of his music.

✻ ✻ ✻ ✻

ANOTHER BRICK IN THE WALL
(PART 1)

Eric Fletcher Waters, was a devout Christian, a member of the Communist Party, and a conscientious objector in the early days of World War II who drove an ambulance during The Blitz. A few years later he would change his mind and join the British Army as an officer of the 8th regiment of the storied Royal Fusiliers infantry.

In December of 1943, British Prime Minister Winston Churchill had a notion how to wrestle control of Rome away from the Axis as he lay recovering from pneumonia. Some even claim the idea came to him in a fever dream. His plan would forever be known as Operation Shingle.

On February 18, 1944, just five months after the birth of his son, Roger, Eric Waters' regiment was tasked with holding a bridgehead at Anzio against a German counterattack led by an awesome force of Tiger tanks. The Royal Fusiliers incurred heavy casualties. Eric Waters was declared missing and eventually presumed dead.

As "Another Brick in the Wall (Part 1)" begins, a synth bass drone drives the "dark." It rises into the mix, carrying an ominous undertone beneath the fading distorted guitar chord. A Hammond organ playing a G Major chord mixes with it like a buzz saw cutting through space and time. Into this journey through Pink's memories comes a single-note picked guitar line, laden with light, ambient echoes symbolic of sound reverberations in an enclosed space. This repetition, not unlike an abstraction of Morse code, subconsciously beacons its message to us. It is no accident that those archaic rhythms of Morse code or even the teletype — both methods of long-distance communication from the not-too-terribly-distant past — pull us into another deep examination of Pink's recollections of youth.

As this G major resolves into a D minor, we slip into a very moody minor key again.

"Another Brick in the Wall (Part 1)" arrives as Pink's dark night of the soul travels to the emotional injuries of his youth. We begin with the scars indelibly left by the death of Pink's (and obviously Roger's) father during the war. In the very first line, Pink talks about his father flown across the ocean. This is the first of many lyrics in *The Wall* involving airplanes and flight and is very significant. Of course, a plane is something that takes you away from one place, but the concept here is taken to the extreme; to Pink, this particular airplane made his father disappear from his life.

Herein is the first brick.

Gilmour punctuates each vocal line with a simple, short guitar lick, each sounding more epic by the fading echoing repetitions of the added delay effect. This is another fine example of the "call and answer" (cause and effect) motif played throughout *The Wall,* which perhaps better serves as a narrative balance more than punctuation.

Echo is very sonically symbolic of the overall concept of human memory throughout *The Wall.* In the second line of the song, the word "memory" is multitracked; this not only sounds incredibly cool, but also serves as a subconscious reminder of the thematic importance of these memories.

Though on the surface it may seem like a minimalistic and simple song, the production here in "Another Brick in the Wall (Part 1)" hides one of the album's most haunting bits of sound design. A very spooky wail can be heard at the third line of the song, after Pink mentions the snapshot of his father in the family album — perhaps the only hard evidence he has that his father even existed. This beautifully rendered analog synthesizer imitates an eerie whistling wind, giving us an aural representation of his father's ghost.

What really makes this so subconsciously effective are the next lyrics in the song: *Daddy, what else did you leave for me?*

Much like the previous lines in the song, this line comes off as a wistful lamentation by young Pink. But as that single distorted guitar hits that big G chord, similar to the one that opens the song, we now get a glimpse at the angst bubbling below Pink's surface. Delivering the echo of the previous line is not childhood Pink any longer; instead it is current-day Pink calling, *Daddy, what d'ya leave behind for me?*

The repetition of this cry for Daddy displays how heavily this question weighs upon Pink's heart. It's no longer about the physical mementos such as old photos or possessions left behind. It's about the effects his father's life may have had upon his own. The painful toll it has taken on him is emphasized here; along with undertones of wondering where this insanity inside him may have come from, Pink's anger and sarcasm clearly asks, "What did you do for me except fuck me up?"

Even deeper, it harkens back to a theme first visited during "The Thin Ice" involving the child having to pay for the sins of the father. Some may recognize the concept of the *inequities of the father visited upon the son* from well-known passages in The Bible (Exodus 20:5, Exodus 34:6-7, Deuteronomy 5:9). If Pink had had an abusive relationship with his father, it would be a simpler situation. By virtue of not knowing his father at all, it's impossible for Pink to ever learn if these emotional difficulties in his life are the product of nature or nurture.

As an absentee father, Pink's daddy still had a very profound impact on his life. Some psychiatric theories clearly state that male children are *born* with the "I want to be daddy" impulse. The belief is that sons, in general, are naturally predisposed to want to become what it is that their father represents to them and that the recognition of this similarity is the basis of all self-identification.

That's some deep shit, especially if that identification and idealization is also the driving mechanism that provides a boy with any sort of grounding in terms of his own masculinity.

If he can't reconcile himself as a man, then who is he?

So, with Pink's father gone and Pink retreating from the real world into his own psychosis, is this in some way his attempt to *disappear* like his father? I'm not talking about being dead, but rather vanishing from view as he hides behind his defense mechanism.

Even more interesting is that despite getting the sense in "The Thin Ice" that Pink's recollections of the past are not happy ones, here in "Another Brick in the Wall (Part 1)" Pink lays the foundation of blame upon someone else for the first time. Reading between the lines, it's a finger-point at his father over the understandable fear of genetic predisposition to insanity.

All in all it was just a brick in the wall.

Right here is the very first mention in the entire album of "The Wall."

At this formative moment in his childhood, as these first bricks are laid, we are treated again to another round of cause and effect. The finger-point of blame is another classic defense mechanism; what makes this time even more trying is that Daddy flew off and never came home, so this particular blame falls upon a ghost. This accounts for the nature of the ethereal and airy audio production choices in this particular song.

Ghosts aren't known for giving answers, so essentially all the introspection over his father's potential role in the mess that is his life will fall hollow at every attempt. There will always be something missing from the search for truth within the fractured relationship he has with what is only a snapshot in a family album.

In the track, there is no actual percussion — not a drum to be heard anywhere. Bringing a pulse to the song, the bass finally makes an appearance at 1:27, but it's not until a few seconds later, at the song's midpoint, where it comes in with any regularity. If you listen to the rhythmic figure it plays, you'll recognize that it is similar to a human heartbeat.

So again, the musical motif of the heartbeat makes an appearance, much like during "In the Flesh?" where the pulse-like renderings of the bass drum keys in on that most natural and universal of human rhythms. The motif of the audible heartbeat is nothing new for Pink Floyd, having prominently used one for both the opening and closing of the entire *Dark Side of The Moon* album. A heartbeat gives us a subconscious association, not only with our own humanity, but going back to our very birth and before: the time our own psychologies are born in the womb. As used in "Another Brick in the Wall (Part 1)," it has a grounding effect not only in our own reality but also in the world outside of the fictional narrative of *The Wall*, emotionally legitimizing the connection we have with Pink's internal struggle.

What follows in "Another Brick in the Wall (Part 1)" is a second half that is both atmospheric and searching in nature. Layered underneath the heartbeat bass and Gilmour's echoing, textured guitar riffs is the unmistakable sound of children at play. Despite a certain innocence in its simplicity and minimalism, there is no feeling of happiness to be found. Pink is not playing along with these other children in his memory. Instead he is an outsider, standing apart from his peers during a time in his life when he was too young to understand enough of the world or what was happening to him.

These are not simple melancholic recollections; these things that have left deep, permanent scars. For Pink, these are the painful memories of not having a father at a time when other children his age had that figure in their lives.

This loss contributes greatly as to why he chooses isolation behind the self-imposed barrier between himself and other humans.

Going back momentarily to the repetitive single guitar note that permeates the entire song — the "Morse code" Gilmour evokes in this message to Pink from his past — it's fairly certain David Gilmour is not playing actual Morse code. The part is made up of only three notes played in succession and then made to sound more repetitive as it is played through a device commonly known as an "echo unit." The effect repeats what Gilmour has played while ping-ponging notes back; those three notes end up sounding like several notes that continue to echo even as Gilmour plays new notes into the device.

The riff, however, is made up of only three notes: one eighth note followed by two sixteenth notes — essentially, one long note followed by two short ones.

Long/short/short...

In Morse code that would be: "- . ." (dash, dot, dot). For whatever coincidence its worth, that sequence is Morse code for the letter "D," the same as the musical key of the song.

If you are more inclined to hear the rhythm of what Gilmour is playing as dot, dot, dash, that would be the Morse code letter "U" (You).

Lastly, it should be noted that one of the reasons "Another Brick in the Wall (Part 1)" imparts a certain shift of feeling is that it's the first song on *The Wall* that is in 4/4 time. Both "In the Flesh?" and "The Thin Ice" are played in 12/8 meter, giving them a decidedly *triplet* feel, whereas "Another Brick in the Wall (Part 1)" has a more common *quadruplet* feel. Though different songs on *The Wall* are performed in different meters to give them different feels from each other, all three parts of "Another Brick In The Wall," though appearing separately on the album, are unified because they all are played in 4/4 time.

✴ ✴ ✴ ✴ ✴

THE HAPPIEST DAYS OF OUR LIVES

Obviously, when it comes to titles, "The Happiest Days of Our Lives" is dripping with sarcasm. This song revisits the twisted mirror duality in *The Wall* where things are not always what they seem from the outside — much like how a physical wall itself can often be used to hide something better left unseen.

There is a lingering darkness to this song as the sound of playing children carried over from "Another Brick In The Wall (Part 1)" fades into the sound of a hovering helicopter, bringing the suggestion of some sort of invasion. The helicopter also brings another evocation of "flight." This time though it carries a connotation of the passage of time; a helicopter is a more modern contrivance than the plane that flew daddy across the ocean, never to return.

The subsequent barking of commands by the schoolteacher — *You! Yes, You! Stand still, laddie!* — undoubtedly adds a more militaristic feeling than one would normally associate with school and those formative years that shape one's perception of the world. The teacher sounds very much like a drill sergeant. This rather overt juxtaposition is clearly an all-out indictment of a system that, much like the military, functions to turn people into obedient drones rather than individual thinkers.

Thus we're transported to something akin to boot camp training meant to strip individuality and make one fall into line. I think there's often an over-fictionalized notion that military indoctrination at the hands of a drill instructor is intended to break you down and then *build you back up*. However, that's not often the case: many will tell you that boot camp serves only to tear you down and then *continue* tearing you down until you are powerless to think for yourself or resist the commands given to you.

Manipulation through intimidation.

It's not an unfair characterization. To understand where Roger Waters is coming from, you have to take a look at how the modern educational system was created. England has had public schools for children going back over a thousand years, but for centuries those schools, both government and church-funded, only served the children of the privileged classes. For common folk, using their children as a source of labor was a far too valuable resource — in many cases, a necessity for survival. But as industry began to grown in western civilization the Statute of Artificers and Apprentices was passed in 1564, forbidding anyone from practicing a trade or craft until they had first served a seven year apprenticeship under a master. Now, all of a sudden, children were being educated as part of learning a trade they would follow for the rest of their lives. As the Industrial Revolution began to take shape in the mid-eighteenth century, entrepreneurs were unhappy with the restrictions of such a long apprenticeship program, especially given the acceleration of modern technologies and the pace required keeping up with growing markets.

Thus, the need for competent workers who were skilled *just* enough — but not too much – became very much a concern for the economic stability and growth of the country. To this end, the Elementary Education Act was passed in 1870, requiring compulsory education for all children between the ages of five and ten, at which point they could enter the workplace.

If you look at the rest of western civilization, you'll see a very similar story and intent. Far from being set up to ever set up to help the individual spirit flourish, the modern educational system was designed simply to create good employees who toe the company line. Indoctrinating these perfect employees required suppression of their individuality, achieved through the systematic exposure of that person's weaknesses. That person then believes they are only as good as their closest authority figure feels they are.

In the case of Pink — and by obvious extension, Roger — you have a school boy who has no father figure, so the only male authority figure in his life is his sadistic schoolteacher. A father figure is supposed to provide discipline and love, but the schoolteacher only knows harsh criticism. Pink, helpless against the cruelties thrust upon him, is forced to enact his defense mechanism and build his wall.

As this authoritarian nightmare figure of the schoolteacher vanishes, once again you have Gilmour's single-note, echo-picked guitar teletyping. As a continued presence, it represents the constant repetition of an idea, almost hypnotically brainwashing the listener with the deep messages built throughout *The Wall*.

Listen to the rhythm of the hi-hat cymbal as it enters the mix, sounding almost like a military snare drum, adding to the authoritarian presence. Again, the song is cut almost directly in half with the lyrical section beginning at the midpoint. Unlike Pink's finger-point at his father for the unhappiness that drives him to isolate himself, the lyrics in "The Happiest Days of Our Lives" do not demonstrate outright blame. Instead they serve to out the teachers as bullies and sadistic assholes. Waters uses very clever psychological techniques of association, brilliantly letting us form the basis for blame in our own minds, possibly even emphasized by the similar feelings we may have about our own educational experiences. This way he can point the finger without actually doing so. Coming from Pink's perspective, this song is a veritable report card on the teachers themselves.

Given the era of Pink/Roger's educational tour of duty, it's probably safe to say that these teachers were former soldiers themselves. These were men who fought "The Hun" in World War I and then "Jerry and Tojo" in World War II. Fast forward a few years later, here they are, unappreciated old codgers who get none of the respect they feel they should have — not even at home from their "fat and psychopathic wives" who "thrash them within inches of their lives."

This motif of bullying that trickles down from the wives to the teachers and then to the children is fascinating because of how perfectly it dovetails into the cyclical narrative of *The Wall*. We are seeing the erosion of Pink's psyche in a case of "what goes around, comes around." Later in the album's second half we'll see the frightening results of the residual effect, but it leaves one to wonder if these teachers are bullies because they themselves were the product of an educational system run by similarly cruel men who infected a new generation with their sickness.

Cause and effect.

There's a great punctuation to this at the end of the lyric ...*exposing every weakness however carefully hidden by the kids.* The schoolteacher's maniacal laughter plays directly to the authoritarian's state of mind, showing a peek at his insanity.

Worth mentioning is the pre-delay effects on Roger Waters' vocal track that cause you to hear ghost echoes of the beginning of each line before the actual vocal comes in. Aside from being a sort of musical "foreshadowing," it adds a *déjà vu* quality to the lyrics. In the pre-computer music mixing days when *The Wall* was recorded, this type of effect was achieved by basically flipping the master tape over, running it backwards through a delay unit then printing that echo onto another track. Once you flip the tape back over, the delay sounds like it happens before the vocal comes in.

Truthfully, "The Happiest Days of Our Lives" is less of a traditional song than it is the connective tissue that ties together "Another Brick In The Wall (Part 1)" and "Another Brick In The Wall (Part 2)." Musically, it even stays in the same tempo, key and meter.

Again, you visit the Dickensian notion *It was the best of times. It was the worst of times.* Here was youth and the beauty of innocent life spoiled as Pink's dignity was robbed when he was too powerless to keep it from happening — stolen by those father figures who abused their power. It's really no wonder Waters juxtaposed the military which killed his father over the similar authoritarian system that poisoned his childhood.

✻ ✻ ✻ ✻ ✻

ANOTHER BRICK IN THE WALL (PART 2)

We don't need no education.
We don't need no thought control.

Equating education with thought control is a hallmark of nearly every major dystopian work of art ever created. One of the true genius elements in "Another Brick in the Wall (Part 2)" is how deeply it draws upon the listener's mental real estate, already occupied by concepts from literary works like Aldous Huxley's seminal *Brave New World,* Ray Bradbury's incendiary *Fahrenheit 451,* and George Orwell's scarily prescient *1984.* What we are seeing here, through Pink's eyes, is how ingraining the prohibition of free thought becomes institutionalized.

Emphasis on the pressure to conform is a very dystopian theme that echoes the ruthless egalitarianism of Kurt Vonnegut's *Harrison Bergeron,* in which people are stigmatized by individual ability or accomplishment or somehow standing out from the herd.

Along with the DNA these dystopian literary gems have their imprinted on *The Wall,* no discussion would be complete without including Franz Kafka's *The Trial.* In Kafka's vision of a future society that commands conformity no matter the cost, Josef K, the protagonist, is arrested upon suspicion of acting in a way unlike how others are expected to act. He has committed no crime, aside from the seemingly heinous act of being an individual. Within Kafka's masterwork we are exposed to K's intense feelings of alienation and anxiety — again, all because he is deemed *different*, isolated from society.

Perhaps more overt within the realm of Roger Waters' overall thematic messages in *The Wall* is this concept of thought control as seen in Orwell's *1984*. Here, a culture of warfare becomes a necessity (and symptom) of the totalitarian rule in order to keep the populace in a constant state of unease. By manipulating with fear, order was kept; citizens did as they were told by the government, without question.

With enough conditioning, people will stop thinking for themselves and fall into the herd for their own safety.

The earlier that conditioning begins, the more docile the populace becomes.

Dystopia.

Hey! Teacher! Leave them kids alone.

Certainly there are no illusions of a utopian life for Pink as a youth. We arrive at "Another Brick in the Wall (Part 2)" after having absorbed the many layers we've been given in *The Wall*'s narrative. The previous track, "The Happiest Days of Our Lives" established the teacher as a monster who inflicts all of the disappointments of his own life upon his pupils. This gives us a tremendous understanding of Pink's youth and the reasoning behind his extremely bleak indictment of the modern educational system. Add the nuance of knowing that the cruel schoolteacher struggles himself with what it's like to be beaten, along with the emotional (and most likely physical) beatings that come full circle from the teacher's wives to a student like Pink, and you are given a radical 360-degree view of the root of the problem.

If you don't eat your meat, you can't have any pudding! How can you have any pudding if you don't eat your meat?

Within the narrative framework of *The Wall,* this line, as voiced in Pink's mind by the schoolteacher, could very well be an echo of the abuse the schoolteacher himself received from the fat and psychopathic wife who thrashes him within inches of his life.

But note that he's not overtly suggesting a way to save this microcosm of the world of modern education. Instead, you are presented with the cause and effect of why this world is busted. And, like Pink himself, it is possible that it is irretrievably broken.

"Another Brick in The Wall (Part 2)" takes a metaphorical right turn with the narrative by finally taking Pink past the questioning of why he is the way he is to a true realization of self. By stating such a strong disdain for the system that caused him such emotional injury, Pink rebels for the first time in his life. He's been a passive victim up to this point, a pinball only acted upon by other influences. Now he rises up, rebellious, symbolizing a defiant generation.

We don't need no education.

We don't need no thought control.

The great irony here is that both of these lines, as metaphorically spoken by the pupils, are grammatically incorrect. Both contain double negatives and in fact would actually mean *we need education and thought control.* Again, the twisted mirror dichotomy appears in a way that warns you to look for the truth beyond the surface.

Revealing the intentions of the state and pulling back the curtain is the very definition of "antiestablismentarianism." In what could be one of the finest examples of rock and roll subversion, this song is a complete indictment of institutionalized conformity rendered in a perfect disco beat.

When the tracks were originally recorded, the song was only made up of a single verse and chorus lasting a mere 1:20 that sounded — as once described by Nick Mason — as rather funereal. Just prior to joining Pink Floyd to record *The Wall*, producer Bob Ezrin had just wrapped recording and mixing Nils Lofgren's eponymously-titled album *Nils*. The process was completed in one room of New York City's famed Record Plant at the same time disco super-producer Nile Rogers was finishing the third album by his smash hit band Chic in another room. That album, *Risqué*, contained three hit singles, including the #1 Billboard chart-topper *Good Times*.

Ezrin insisted on a commercial single from *The Wall*, and so he turned his ear to the funk inflections of Gilmour's rhythm guitar part. Ezrin began a scheme to turn "Another Brick in the Wall (Part 2)" into that radio-ready single by first marrying the current track to a Chic-like drum groove. After determining that 103 beats per minute was the perfect tempo for a dance song, Ezrin then coerced drummer Nick Mason to play the kind of plodding four-on-the-floor rhythm needed to make it happen.

Razor blade in hand, Ezrin copied the first chorus to the end of the song and then added some drum fills. But he wasn't done. He soon came up with a brilliant idea that would become the song's most signature motif.

Having previously worked with Goth-rock godfather Alice Cooper on the smash single, *School's Out,* Ezrin knew there was immense psychological power in the use of children's voices in songs that were critical of education. While Ezrin and Waters were in Los Angeles overseeing the recording of the orchestral parts and other assorted overdubs, recording engineer Nick Griffiths was sent to Islington Green School, which just happened to be down the road from the band's own Brittania Row Studios in North London. There Griffiths found a willing accomplice in music teacher Alun Renshaw, who enlisted twenty three students, ages eleven to sixteen, to sing in exchange for getting Brittania Row to professionally record Islington Green's orchestra. In true, anti-establishment tradition, teacher Renshaw did the whole thing without telling the school's headmistress.

The whole session with the students took only one forty-minute class session to track the chorus vocals a dozen times. Later, after word got out, some people were outraged that these poor schoolchildren were being exploited by millionaire rock stars and a deal was eventually struck that would financially benefit the school.

Initially, Waters was reluctant to the idea. However, once he heard the youthful and edgy addition of the cockney and posh children's voices in the mix, he recognized how important this song would eventually become.

Even though he wasn't a co-writer on "Another Brick in The Wall (Part 2)," it would be hard to dismiss David Gilmour's contribution to the psychological undertow of the song. Aside from the funk-infused clean, effected, flanged guitar in the rhythm track, Gilmour's solo here exhibits a raw sense of individuality in the second half of the song, as if striving to voice its artistic self among the institutionalized essence of the disco beat. Using a '55 Les Paul Gold Top through the neck pickup, Gilmour renders this solo in these modular sections that syncopated in between the beat, giving it a real funky feel. Amidst the subtext of the Hammond organ holding down these long church-like chords, it really feels like the guitar is testifying to the realization of having one's own voice and individuality. It is one guitar, speaking up.

In early 1980, when "Another Brick in The Wall (Part 2)" was released as a single, the lyrical stance of the song created quite a bit of knee-jerk controversy. In response, Waters stated that the song didn't stand in opposition to all education, only to that which closes the minds of children instead of opening them. It would be impossible to discount the possibility that he said that only to placate those for whom a metaphor — or the ability to see anything in context — requires far too much mental heavy lifting.

Successful artists are capable of locating humanity's pulse and somehow distilling raw emotions from it. They are the observers of our time, responsible for seeing more of the truth than the rest of us, who are trapped within the confines of our own lives.

Back in the 1970's (and up until it was formally abolished in 1990) South Africa had a system of racial segregation in place formally known as "apartheid." Aside from being denied civil rights, the lives of black South Africans were controlled by the white ruling party made up of the descendants of European colonists.

Opposition to apartheid was evident at every level of South Africa's black society, but nowhere was it as vocal as the student population. In 1974, the country's all-white government passed the Afrikaans Medium Decree, forcing all black schools to deliver at least half of all school instruction in the Dutch-derived language of Afrikaans. While English would be utilized for most of the rest of the curriculum, it was the indigenous languages that were banned from all studies aside from religion, music and physical culture.

The significance of forcing Afrikaans upon the blacks of South Africa had everything to do with the efforts of the white ruling party to continue to industrialize the country. Under apartheid, a black man could never expect to rise above the level of laborer and, much like the efforts centuries earlier to create a system of education in order to produce capable employees, they had to be able to understand the language of their bosses.

On June 16, 1976, black teenagers from the Johannesburg neighborhood of Soweto took to the streets in protest. When the police couldn't control the crowds with tear gas and attack dogs, they opened fire upon the students with live ammunition. As the smoke cleared, the government claimed the "official" casualty count stood at 23 killed. It was later revealed that in fact roughly 700 people lost their lives and another 4,000 were left injured.

And though it's never been publicly stated by Waters that the Soweto school massacre had any direct influence upon "Another Brick in The Wall (Part 2)," it's easy to see how such a tragic event that outraged the world could have made an impact on him. Most certainly Water's awesome bird-of-prey screech, vocalized at the very beginning of the song, warns of immediate danger coming our way.

"Another Brick in The Wall (Part 2)" was adopted by black students across South Africa as an anthem against their school system. The government responded by banning both the song and *The Wall*. Though it took time, in the end, the government fell anyway.

❈ ❈ ❈ ❈

MOTHER

As a child, when you are hurt or you are scared, you cry out to mother. Mother is the one who will be there to protect you.

Every single human being, at some point, has a mother.

Exposed in Pink's youth, "Mother" demonstrates the daring wide-eyed innocence from a boy who has been threatened his whole life with the prospect of World War III. Here he delves back into the past, to the other major figure he holds responsible for what has become of his emotional state. The song begins with the sound of a deep inhale and exhale.

Is it from relief?

Doubtful. It is instead more like the anxiety that hits in the moment before you're about to approach someone with hard questions. Yet, because children usually aren't filled with self-anguish before throwing out the hard-to-answer questions of life, it doesn't seem like a thing a child would do. This suggests that the exhale we hear comes from adult Pink in the moment before his flashback begins.

When Pink begins singing, his voice is calm. His questions are very young at the beginning and show a progression of life's wisdom. Each subsequent question seems to come from a slightly older Pink. What this means is we're in essence watching Pink grow up while we listen; yet at no time do we see him depart from mother's shadow.

One thing remains true throughout: none of the questions posed to Pink's mother can ever be truly answered. Any answer given would have zero effect whether or not the thing in question happened (Mother, do you think they'll drop the bomb?).

Every single question asked to Mother is hypothetical.

Psychologists who have studied the effects of modern advertising, especially political advertising, have discovered that constant exposure to hypothetical questions causes a "mental contamination" in the human mind. When the psyche is overwhelmed with the unanswerable, it becomes vulnerable to subconscious mental processing that is both uncontrollable and causes unwanted judgment, behavior or emotion.

As adult Pink's brain has hit the point where he finds himself confronted with this raw self-evaluation during this dark night of the soul, he seeks answers in his past for all of his own unwanted judgment, behavior and emotion. It's no wonder that as we see this parallel of Pink growing bit by bit with each question, his neurosis is further demonstrated by this laundry list of hypothetical questions. Once more, we see both cause and effect — first by our understanding of what Pink is mentally going through as we come into this song, and then by the further revelation of what caused his broken psyche.

Thematically speaking, it's a bold statement about the negative effects of constant worry over the things in life over which you have little or no control.

When Pink's voice briefly loses that calm veneer and grows more frenetic during the question of whether or not he'll end up on the firing line, echoing his fear over war and ending up like his father, he is essentially asking "Will I have to be brave?"

You can almost see Pink sitting on his bed, growing up and strumming these chords alone, arriving at what is arguably the greatest existential question of all:

Is it just a waste of time?

How mother responds becomes an interesting and telling dynamic.

During the verse, the time signature of "Mother" is a slightly non-conformist 5/8, as opposed to the more standard 4/4 we've been in during the previous three songs. However, when we get to the chorus of the song — made up of Gilmour singing Pink's recollections of Mother's responses — we fall back into the same 12/8 meter used the last time we visited Mother during "The Thin Ice." Not only does this musically tie us back to that previous moment in the narrative, but the triplet feel (1, 2, 3... 1, 2, 3...) evokes almost a fast waltz; Mother has a way of dancing around the questions.

Melodically speaking, Mother's response sounds like a lullaby. It even begins lyrically like one.

Hush now, baby. Baby don't you cry...

Much as in "The Thin Ice," Mother's responses don't actually answer any of Pink's questions. Instead, the nature of the lyrics reveal what Pink's mother means to him.

Mother represents a certain type of truth in Pink's twisted world. Despite Mother's overprotective overcompensation (perhaps from the parental unwillingness to allow their kids to grow up in their own eyes), here in his mind, she knows all.

Mama will make it all better. Mama will keep you safe.

He needs her approval. He needs her to tell him it will be all right. He needs her to help him make up his mind about who he is even though, in the twisted mirror of truth, he knows Mother has unintentionally messed him up because of her overprotection.

Number of times the word "mother" is used: 12.

Number of times "baby" or "babe" is mentioned: 9.

At first, she refers to him as "baby," in the same way you would when a child is a baby. But then it changes to "babe," which goes a long way towards demonstrating most parents' inability to ever see their children as anything other than their baby.

In addition, note when we hear Pink's recollection of mother's voice as sung by David Gilmour: she refers to herself only as "mama," which is one of the first (if not *the very* first) word that infants learn to speak.

Number of times the word "mama" is sung: 10.

Under the chorus there is this wonderful pastoral Anglican style organ playing that functions as a counterpoint to the anxiety. Subliminally it deifies Mother by helping her response sound almost holy. However, when you take into account the weight of the unanswerable questions being posed and the evasive non-answers being given by "mama," you almost get the sense that "Mother" is also a cleverly-veiled commentary on his views of religion or big government —essentially lambasting any sort of organized institution that uses fear as a tool to control the masses.

Mama's gonna put all of her fears into you…

Perhaps noteworthy is that Roger Waters has told people that his own mother was a communist. How influential this is upon the type of responses Mother gives in the chorus depends upon your view of how much propaganda "mama" is trying to tell her boy.

When we get into the second verse, we're with a much older Pink, one who now needs to run to mother in order to help him define what love means.

Mother, do you think she's good enough — for me?

Mother, do you think she's dangerous — to me?

We even get the frenetic Pink voice once again revealing the true motive of the questions.

Mother, will she tear your little boy apart?

For an overprotective mother, how much more of a loaded question could you ask?

Ooooh aaah. Mother, will she break my heart?

In the first verse, when he asks if she thinks they'll drop the bomb or put him on that firing line, we're seeing his childhood fear of the overarching menace of global military war, especially as it was the cause of his father's death. But here, we sense his fear of emotional war, and by extension, fear of intimacy.

The Freudian connotations at play in Pink's recollections as a young adult become evident. According to Freud, a child's identification with the same-sex parent is the successful resolution of the Oedipus complex — a son's desire to eliminate the father in order to possess the mother. Unsuccessful resolutions might lead to neurosis. Complete inability to resolve the father-son relationship is conducive to a boy becoming an aggressive, over-ambitious, and vain man.

Perhaps like a rock star who spits into the face of an out-of-control audience member?

Even the title, "Mother," seems like an offhand nod to the influence of Freudian psychological theories in the overall narrative of Pink's undoing — especially when it comes to the way Mother implies she will be the only woman he needs in his life.

Mama's gonna keep baby healthy and clean.

Consider this: *The Wall* was released in November of 1979 and John Lennon's *Plastic Ono Band* album was released in December of 1970; both hugely influential albums became the great rock and roll bookends of that decade.

The *Plastic Ono Band* album also features a song called "Mother," released as a single after the smash hit of "Instant Karma." John Lennon's "Mother" is a haunting and emotionally raw lament penned to his parents who both abandoned him during his childhood. John's father, as it would turn out, left the family when John was merely an infant. Although they were close, John's mother did not live with him while he was growing up. She would later be killed by a drunk-driving off-duty police officer when John was just seventeen.

The song starts with the tolling of church bells. In the second verse, John sings "Father, you left me, but I never left you…"

In the bridge he sings, "Mamma don't go…Daddy come home…" and then later on, "Goodbye… Goodbye…"

Given the massive popular appeal of John Lennon during that time, one could easily assume that Roger Waters was aware of the *Plastic Ono Band* album, and given the direct parallels between the emotions John lays out bare in his "Mother," it would seem like the type of song that would resonate in Roger's own life.

In Pink's world, mother shut him off from the rest of the world. Due to her enabling, she is an accomplice to the building of the wall. She had her chance to help prevent it when he asked her permission.

Ooooo. Mother, should I build the wall?

And yet we know that he built it and it is only now, in his adult life, that he painfully sees her complicity in the act of his self-imprisonment. As an adult, if Mother — his protector! — is gone, he is now left alone and unable to fend for himself.

Which leaves us on the most hypothetical question of all in Pink's world:

Mother did it need to be so high?

❈ ❈ ❈ ❈ ❈

GOODBYE BLUE SKY

If you have ever experienced hearing Word War II airplanes taking wing above you, you have no doubt that the dusky rumble of those engines has an aural signature all its own. Even today, decades after driving Tojo and the Hun to their surrender, lucky vintage flyers still pilot a handful of these surviving craft on weekends and during air shows. The house where I currently live in Los Angeles places me underneath a certain flight path that seems to carry World War II-era planes over my roof with a reasonably impressive frequency. It has not been uncommon, on a hot summer afternoon, to hear those engines approaching from far in the sky and to find me sprinting from whatever I may be doing inside the house, through the patio door and into the backyard, to hopefully catch a glimpse of a Corsair, Spitfire, the occasional B-17 or the very rare Zero.

Between living my entire life in and around populated urban and suburban areas, and having once worked in an office situated at the Santa Monica Airport, I've heard my share of airplane engines. I can tell you without hesitation that, regardless of the vintage or the technology involved, propeller-driven planes from World War II sound like nothing else. Their pistons groan with a throaty roar that seems to resonate a half-octave lower than anything made today.

The opening seconds of this track bring us a perfect tranquility. Birds sing in the trees. Everything seems so peaceful and clean.

Then rising into the mix comes the sound of such an airplane overhead: a pistoned war bird.

Look mummy, there's an aero-plane up in the sky… chimes the voice of a small child (voiced by none other than Roger's son, Harry). A symbolic moment of life's innocence – and we are here now to bid it farewell.

Sometime around *The Wall*'s initial release in 1979, Roger Waters described "Goodbye Blue Sky" as the summation of Pink's life up to this point. "It's remembering one's childhood and then getting ready to set off into the rest of one's life," he said.

One of the things that help *The Wall* subliminally resonate as a narrative is how it very much parallels a classic three-act structure used in movie storytelling. Generally, in the first act, you establish your protagonist by entering his or her life during the normal moment before the event that changes things. By the end of the first act, the protagonist metaphorically (and sometimes physically) "leaves home." This is the beginning of the journey where the story's protagonist takes his life experiences and finally has to act and make choices. As Pink's previously-eroding psyche has finally begun to come undone and he enters into this dark night of the soul, "Goodbye Blue Sky" marks the beginning of act two. He says goodbye to innocence and, in the absence of the father who was never there, has to take that first step from the nest to learn what it is to be a man.

The first musical instrument we hear is a very organic-sounding nylon string acoustic guitar. Its finger-picked notes resonate clearly for four bars until it is joined by a very synthetic-sounding bass drone. This in itself is an audio metaphor for the organic versus the mechanical. That synthesizer's ominous tone rumbles at a very similar frequency to that of the airplane we hear enter the mix during the intro. The finger-picked guitar represents the carefree song of the humble bird, oblivious to man's mundane problems — even as the blue sky is blotted out by planes intended as tools for war.

Di', di, di', did you see the frightened ones?
Di', di, di', did you see the falling bombs?

Pink is clearly coming to understand that life is not all rainbows and skittles.

Interestingly enough, in "Mother" he asks if they're going to drop the bomb. Here he clearly believes bombs have been dropped, yet his asking makes it seem as if he's *not* quite sure and needs reassurance from someone else that it actually happened.

It's probably safe to say that in "Mother," by asking if she thinks they'll drop *the* bomb, instead of just any bomb, he's referring to a nuclear weapon of mass destruction and potentially the end of the world. In "Goodbye Blue Sky," the reference is aimed towards evoking the nature of war itself and the terrible bombing that turned a great portion of London into rubble during World War II. Waters has said that his father, before going off to fight and die in the war, was a conscientious objector who drove an ambulance during the Blitz, which was an extended campaign of strategic bombing of England by the Germans for several months over 1940 and 1941. For an almost mind-boggling fifty seven straight nights, the Luftwaffe bombed London. Over one million homes and buildings were destroyed and 40,000 men, women and children lost their lives.

Death from above, indeed.

Thus, a juxtaposition at the beginning of this song: the voice of an innocent child gazing in wide wonder at the airplane in the sky that will end his innocence. The lyrics speak of the destruction of war through the eyes of a child growing in fear. His "Did, did, did you see" come as a stutter.

Di' di' di' did you ever wonder why we had to run for shelter
When the promise of a brave, new world unfurled beneath the clear blue sky?

Given the thematic elements here in "Goodbye Blue Sky," it's very organic to mention shelter in the wake of the threat of bombs. From World War II throughout the cold war, the presence of bomb shelters was not uncommon in major cities like London and well into the suburbs. There's an interesting bit of connective tissue here that leads to another major dystopian literary work that Waters cleverly name drops without being too overt: Aldous Huxley's *Brave New World*.

Huxley's novel delves deeply into the catastrophic aftermath of a society that has embraced the conceits of Futurism. The glory of technology, speed, youth, and violence as a social movement becomes the unquestioned norm and leads to the betrayal of humanity by the creation of assembly lines. In trying to achieve personal satisfaction through technology, mankind undermines the very precepts of civilization. In *Brave New World*, personal interaction has been devalued to the point that the very essence of civility has crumbled. The perversion of this utopian search for peace and social stability has rendered the world devoid of love, beauty, and true relationships. Even emotion has no place in this new world.

This sort of assembly-line mentality is exactly what Pink has encountered in the educational system.

Even more sinister in *Brave New World*, babies are spawned in laboratory test tubes in order to be born perfect. The idea of creating a master race of children free of defect evokes shades of Hitler's own master plan. Rest assured, we haven't seen the last of the malformed ghosts of fascist ideals in *The Wall;* they will rear their ugly heads during the album's second half.

With this one mention of *Brave New World* — a work that, much like *The Wall*, uses the dangerous effects of separation and isolation as thematic elements — Waters is able to very cleverly plant this seed and foreshadow what is growing inside of Pink's paranoia. Here, even as he talks about the evil of others, Pink cannot see this growing darkness of his own shadow self.

The flames are all long gone, but the pain lingers on.

Seeing that plane, possibly similar to the one in which "daddy flew across the ocean," must have an effect on Pink and the scars of his youth. He is a victim of a war on two fronts: the real battles waged between civilizations and the war waged with oneself for sanity.

Not only does Pink bidding farewell to the "blue sky" work as a metaphor for his childhood innocence becoming overcast with gloom as he is about to leave the nest, but it also speaks to his inability to look up at a beautiful peaceful sky the same way again. For Pink, the sky brings death and it takes away those he loves.

After the final "Goodbye," the song fades into the ambient sounds of an airport terminal. Pink is traveling ahead to a later stage in life and, as we will continue to see, when you travel you sometimes leave behind the ones you love.

* * * * *

EMPTY SPACES

The ghostly wisps of airport terminal ambience and faces from the past fade; the journey now reaches at its next destination. Our arrival point now pulsates with a mechanical rhythm conveying the essence an assembly line of some sort. The synth and guitar play a subdued, darker, much more sinister version of "In the Flesh."

In many regards, this industrial throbbing percussion in "Empty Spaces" makes the song feel like a blood cousin to "Welcome to the Machine" from the band's smash album *Wish You Were Here.* Even lyrics from "Welcome to the Machine" seem to echo from the same DNA of disillusionment found throughout *The Wall.*

What did you dream? It's alright. We told you what to dream.

The musical separation from the living, breathing, organic sound of the finger-picked acoustic nylon-string guitar of "Goodbye Blue Sky" to this synth-driven conveyor belt heightens the sense that we have been torn from the innocence of Pink's youth. There is no more free pass from obligation that childhood often affords us. Now, as a young adult, Pink is faced with the obligations of manhood.

Primarily those which come with romantic entanglements.

Is this some sort of Brave New World for Pink? Is this a world filled with the Futurist's embrace of technology that separates us from our loved ones and, more dangerously, ourselves?

Narratively-speaking, Pink now remembers himself as a young adult. The years have not been kind. Throughout his upbringing, his unstable relationship with his own place in the world has deeply affected his ability to connect with others and form true relationships.

Is he now paying dearly for it, because inside of his soul he now feels these "Empty Spaces?"

As a work that deals with the erosion of sanity and its effects upon relationships, *The Wall* contains surprisingly few overt references to Syd Barrett, the founding member whose LSD addiction fried his brain and forced him out of the band. Perhaps Roger felt he had excised Syd's spirit with *Wish You Were Here*'s infamous ode to Syd, "Shine on You Crazy Diamond."

That being said, there are moments in *The Wall* that feel like we are being visited briefly by the ghost of Syd's presence in the band and in Roger's life. Remember, Syd was Pink Floyd's original lead singer and songwriter; it was only after Syd's mental breakdown and subsequent curb-kicking that Roger began his brilliant career as a songwriter. In this case, however, it's not so much a visit from Syd's ghost as an embodiment of the man but instead as a form of cautionary tale.

"Empty Spaces" is a song about failed communication.

What shall we use to fill the empty spaces where we used to talk?

Of all the clichéd audio trickery allegedly found in rock record audio production of the era, backmasking was not a Pink Floyd hallmark. This practice of searching for backwards messages, intentionally inserted into recorded music in order to deliver a subliminal message, really didn't hit the mainstream until 1969 when a caller at a Detroit rock radio station convinced disc jockey Russ Gibb to play The Beatles' "Revolution 9" in reverse. Therein, explained the caller, were clues to prove the rumors of Paul McCartney's death were indeed true. When played backwards, the phrase "Number nine" became obvious — to some people — as "turn me on dead man." When other listeners tried this sonic experiment on their turntables at home, the station's switchboards lit up. According to them, the mix also contained buried, backwards recordings of a car crash and the voice of someone screaming, "Let me out!"

Record companies and artists scoffed, citing the phenomenon of "phonetic reversal," wherein a word sounds like another word when reversed. This did not deter some rabid backmasking hunters from convincing themselves that these subliminal messages were not only subversive in nature, but also boldly satanic.

Possibly one of the greatest examples of backmasking paranoia stems from claims that one of the most famous rock songs ever recorded, "Stairway to Heaven," is filled with backwards praise of the devil himself.

Right after the bridge of "Stairway" Robert Plant sings:

If there's a bustle in your hedgerow, don't be alarmed now
It's just a spring clean for the May queen
Yes, there are two paths you can go by, but in the long run
There's still time to change the road you're on

Without getting too analytical about the lyrics within the context of the song, "Stairway to Heaven" is really about a spirit quest of sorts, harkening back to legendary pursuits like King Arthur's grail quest or Homer's *Iliad*.

The mythical quality of the song's narrative also lends itself to shades of Paganism. The reference to the May Queen invokes an ancient ritual in which a virgin clad in white was chosen to lead a parade for May Day in celebration of spring. After being crowned with flowers though, a sinister fate awaits our lovely May Queen — for in this pagan ritual, she becomes the victim of human sacrifice.

Also quite undeniable is the allusion that the two paths and the choice to change one's road refers to the spiritual destination that awaits at the end of this long journey.

That being said, it's probably not that ridiculous to understand why some self-appointed backmasking detectives believe that when this section of the song is played in reverse, you clearly hear is:

Oh, here's to my sweet Satan

The one whose little path would make me sad, whose power is Satan

He will give those with him 666

There was a little tool shed where he made us suffer, sad Satan

Before you give yourself severe ocular strain from rolling your eyes too hard, take a listen for yourself. (It probably helps to be really high when you do.) Most likely you will find these supposed backwards lyrics to be the product of overactive imaginations belonging to those who strive to find something hidden where nothing exists.

What makes this all very interesting is that "Empty Spaces," a song about failed communication, actually does contain its own backmasking!

Essentially a joke of Roger Waters' own creation, it contains a certain poignancy that helps give this song a very deep meaning within the context of Pink Floyd's history and the tragic story of Syd Barrett.

Beginning at approximately 1:12 into the song there is an obviously unhidden garbled audio element in the mix. Played backwards you can clearly hear what is being said.

"Hello looker," Roger Waters begins. "Congratulations. You have just discovered the secret message. Please send your answer to Old Pink in care of the Funny Farm, Chalfont…"

Then cutting him off before he can deliver the entire address you hear recording engineer James Guthrie call out, "Roger! Carolyne's on the phone!"

To which Roger replies, "Okay."

Considering that original Floyd singer Syd Barrett had been institutionalized in a mental hospital, it's easy to see how this could refer to him, though not as lovingly as in "Shine On You Crazy Diamond."

The "Carolyne" in question is no doubt Carolyne Waters, Roger's second wife. In the past, Waters has publicly stated that if it had not been for Carolyne's insistence on communication between them, he would have ended up as crazy as Pink.

Or perhaps Syd.

It's worth mentioning that the use of Roger's real wife's name is the first time we are removed from *The Wall*'s fictional universe by something directly from the real world. However, that may be precisely the point. In order to illustrate the many layers in *The Wall* and to momentarily remind us that it's a metaphor, he uses

Carolyne as a grounding point to give us the right perspective and see the work for what it is.

* * * * *

YOUNG LUST

I am just a new boy
Stranger in this town...
Where are all the good times.
Who's going to show this stranger around?

Denied innocence unleashed. Released after a lifetime of repression, Pink enters into this raw and unfiltered view of rock and roll's backstage life. I suppose another name for "Young Lust" could just as easily be "Casual Sex in E minor." Hedonism drips from every note; the only thing missing here is the grotto at the Playboy Mansion.

This is Pink unchained through an ejaculation of the soul — so to speak.

More accurately, this is the unchaining of Pink's Id. Again, as we first did (appropriately enough) in "Mother," we delve deep into the Freudian aspects of *The Wall.*

Id, Ego and Super-Ego, according to Freud, make up the three parts of the human psyche. Working backwards, *Super-Ego* is our conscience. It effectively takes the place of past authority figures — such as parents, teachers and other ideal models — and strives to bring perfection to our lives by punishing our misbehavior with feelings of guilt or self-disappointment. *Ego* is what we would essentially call our reason and common sense. Ego wants us to have those things we desire, but in ways that benefit us over the long run as opposed to causing us immediate harm. We derive our human defense mechanisms from Ego, such as denial, fantasy, repression, regression and the other behaviors that cause us to erect barriers between ourselves and others.

But "Young Lust" is all about the Id, that oft-hidden part of our psyche. The Id is a cauldron of seething expectations that wants what it wants, like a newborn child that screams for every desire and impulse and requires immediate satisfaction. Driven by Freud's "Pleasure Principle," the Id seeks to find pleasure (while avoiding pain) in order to sate biological and psychological desires. The Id sits in the driver's seat of the libido, the primary human instinctual force and one that is often unresponsive to the strict demands of reality. In this respect, the Id brings much chaos.

Then again, Pink doesn't live in reality. He has wealth, adoring fans, groupies and physical possessions. He is like a kid in a hyper-sexualized candy store of rock stardom.

Oooooh, I need a dirty woman…
Oooooh, I need a dirty girl.

Now with Pink's Ego too busy constructing and fortifying its defense mechanisms, his Id is allowed to go unchecked.

Reflecting back once more to the song "Welcome to the Machine" from Pink Floyd's album *Wish You Were Here,* we are well aware of the disdain Roger Waters feels for the record industry and the disillusionment it creates. There's a lyric in the song which speaks directly to the rebellion involved to get accepted into the vaunted halls of professional music stardom.

You bought a guitar to punish your ma, you didn't like school, and you know you're nobody's fool…

Given that Waters has publicly described his own mother as having been brought up as a communist, one can only imagine what she must have thought about his choice of a career and the lifestyle it brought.

Oooooh, I need a dirty woman…

The repetition of this need shows his defiance of his Super-Ego's maternal legacy.

By extension, for Pink, the act of becoming a rock star is pure rebellion. Mother is the one who swore she wouldn't let anyone dirty get through. Now look at him. Within the psychosexual framework of the Madonna versus the Whore, you have Pink in search of a girl who is the opposite of his mother.

With no Ego to hold him back or Super-Ego to rationalize his behavior, "Young Lust" represents an experimental phase for Pink, with him leaving his comfort zone and creating a new one — albeit one filled with obvious physical comforts used as surrogates for the emotional comforts he truly desires. Remember that it is Love, a pure human connection, which Pink truly wants. The groupies are just distractions. Rock stars are adored and worshipped by thousands of fans at a time and surrounded by sycophants. Pink is self-medicating with drugs and sex so he won't feel the ravages of loneliness and disconnect. Though he can fill these primal needs, they are still only hollow experiences which don't allow him to create an identity for himself and ultimately don't make him happy.

If Pink feels guilt for his infidelity to the woman with whom he shares those devastating "Empty Spaces," it doesn't show. It is only at the end of the song that Pink's Ego checks in. With the need to reach out to the woman he truly loves, Pink phones home, only to have his transatlantic call answered by the voice of another man.

Despite the irony of his Id's willing abandon to place him waist deep in groupies, it is the Ego that now shatters at the soul-rocking discovery of his love's infidelity.

The phone call, though re-enacted, was inspired by an incident from the band's *In The Flesh* tour where Roger called his first wife Judy and a man answered. That's how he discovered she was cheating on him.

There's a great story behind the recording of the dialogue with the operator. Recording Engineer James Guthrie was working on the album in Los Angeles. Wanting true realism for the bit, he pre-arranged a transatlantic collect call to a neighbor back in London who knew not to accept the charges and instead rudely hang up the phone as if he'd been caught cheating with the caller's wife. The operator would not be told she was being recorded. The first attempt didn't go quite as well as they had hoped. Luckily on the second call they hit pay dirt and recorded the exchange heard on the album. If the operator ever found out her voice was used on *The Wall,* she has yet to come forward to claim her fame.

It seems appropriate that the only bit of true documentarian realism in the entire song about Pink's fictionalized world is, in fact, a prank phone call.

It's also the use of this prank call (the prank was on the operator) that serves as a casual warning for us, the listeners, to remain on our toes.

Musically speaking, the "welcome to the rock and roll circus" atmosphere is vividly enhanced by the way that the musical arrangement to "Young Lust" is a complete homage to the sexualized hard rock songs of the era. Gilmour puts extra grit in his voice, giving the vocals more of an edge along with the Deep Purple/

Jon Lord Hammond organ prevalent in the pre-chorus and chorus. Even the shouting during the solo sounds like rock cliché, not to mention the Rick Derringer-esque guitar lick at the end of the second verse that sounds like something lifted from "Rock and Roll Hoochie Koo."

Short of being considered parody, Waters has himself described "Young Lust" as a "pastiche" — a work of art that openly imitates the work of a previous artist, sometimes with the intent of satire.

What Weird Al Yankovic does can be described as *pastiche*. But then again, because it includes so many different distinct styles based upon famous previous works of art, Queen's "Bohemian Rhapsody" qualifies as a pastiche as well. One could actually apply the *pastiche* moniker to the movie *Star Wars* as well, given that creator George Lucas borrowed heavily from the traditional science fiction books, movies and television shows of his youth. Cinematically-speaking, there is possibly no greater practitioner of the modern *pastiche* today than Quentin Tarantino.

Just because something is a pastiche doesn't mean it is an inferior work. By artfully creating a work that stands on its own, while at the same time invoking some of the pop-cultural shorthand we've grown up with, a pastiche can rightfully exist as a singular effort and even rise above others.

The one very fascinating aspect to rendering this song as such a pastiche is that it speaks to Pink's individuality. It goes to show that he has not yet developed into his own man, an independent artist, but instead lives as an avatar whose life is crudely made up of every rock cliché in the book.

✶ ✶ ✶ ✶ ✶

ONE OF MY TURNS

He is a bag of meat — exposed to the world. Every normal defense mechanism that would allow him to remain within the outside world has failed him. Metaphorically naked and vulnerable to injury, Pink builds a protective wall to hide behind.

But is he fooling himself into believing his isolation is strength?

In some respects you have to wonder if Ernest Hemingway did any favors for artists with his book *The Old Man and the Sea*. His protagonist is completely isolated from people by his choice to spend so much time on the ocean. The "Old Man" is defined by this isolation. He suffers from a longing and loneliness which take a toll on him emotionally, wearing down his humanity. In the same regard, it is this same suffering that Hemingway uses as the manna that nourishes a part of his soul and gives him the strength to fight the epic battles with the fish he catches. It's not beyond the old man to accept (or admit he needs) help from other people; however this resolve allows him to fight the mighty marlin he uses to define his ultimate sense of being and character.

He is a man because he suffers for his craft.

Obviously, with Pink, as would be with many other artists, solitude is a necessity for the development of a unique identity capable of creating art with a unique voice. But in implying that such great solitude is the necessary tool to do battle with the big catch, has Hemingway romanticized this notion of solitude to the point where those incapable of seeing they are in trouble use it as justification to suffer needlessly?

Is this battle Pink fights with his own solitude justified in his mind as a hardship similar to the battles his father faced (and ultimately lost) in the war? Could it be that his acceptance to fall further into despair is his trial in order to attain manhood?

If so, he is failing and doesn't yet realize the danger he is, both to himself and others around him.

Previously, in "Young Lust," we found Pink plunging head-long into hedonistic waters. Now he is left with nothing but a dial tone. Much like Pink's life, there is nobody on the other end of this connection.

Mother do you think they'll drop the bomb?

Pink has certainly just had one dropped on him; however, unlike the bomb that killed Pink's father at the Anzio bridgehead, this one has dealt him the soul-destroying blow of illuminating his wife's infidelity. Blindsided by the reality of hearing another man pick up his phone, Pink is sent into a completely stunned silence.

Like Ebenezer Scrooge, another man who justified his own isolation as a necessity, it is time for Pink to get a visit from his own Ghost of Christmas Present.

For the first time since the opening strains of "In the Flesh?" we return to present day. Interestingly, the groupie gets her own voice and, like the telephone operator in "Young Lust," she is not a not a simply a voice created by someone in the band or by Pink's own psyche. She is separate from Pink's past. These voices belong to Pink's here and now.

Given the constant use of duality from both sides of the twisted mirror (showing what is real and what isn't), the juxtaposition of the groupie's voice over that of the TV actors gives us the unspoken sense that she is just a part in his play.

Roger Waters was obviously aware that, as an album, *The Wall* would be consumed not only as a whole — played from beginning to end without interruption — but also in pieces, often out of context with each other. The narrative that he has so carefully crafted would inevitably be broken by those who sample only pieces of the greater work. Therefore, in order to make each piece still work, each was created to be self-referential (though sometimes in ways that seem merely subliminal). A listener whose knowledge of the story has grown by consuming all of the previous songs on the album to this point gets more from his emotional investment, yet someone who has just joined the work in progress can still pick up on these subtle shades of story.

What we get in the first fifty-six seconds of this song is just dialogue from this groupie, yet it paints a fairly clear picture of Pink. He's a rich rock star holed up in a giant suite. He is unresponsive to the groupie, ignoring even her salacious come on to get naked with her. Pink instead chooses to sit and vegetate in the numbing glow of classic shows and movies on the television.

The narrative of her dialogue is no accident, but brilliantly rendered to foreshadow coming lyrics in the song.

Wow. Look at this fabulous room!
Are all these your guitars?
Can I get a drink of water?

Wanna take a bath?
What are you watching?
And possibly the most telling of all:
Are you feeling okay?
Wow. What a loaded question. How little the unsuspecting groupie knows about Pink! The answer, as she is about to find out for herself, is a resounding "no." As Pink's turns go, this is obviously one for the worse. He has just suffered a tremendous blow. His wife is no longer in love with him, though he still loves her. Moreover, he *needs* her. It's possible that she was the last lifeline to what was real in his life, the lone tether to sanity. It's as if this relationship has smashed into a wall.

Pink now relinquishes the unabashed control of his life by his Id and retreats into his Ego as defense mechanisms come up between him, the groupie he brought back to his room, and in fact with the rest of the real world. According to Freud, there are several levels of defense mechanisms that occur in the human psyche. The first and second levels are what Freud termed the "pathological" and "immature" levels. What Pink experiences here are more along the lines of a level three defense mechanism: feelings of Isolation, Dissociation and severe Repression. These are known as "neurotic" defense mechanisms and only provide short-term coping.

In some regards, Pink is going through the first stage of grief: shock and denial. He is numbed by disbelief. Inside, Pink is a seething cauldron of emotions, though on the outside he seems completely distant. He remains transfixed by the old movie playing on the TV and it's easy to understand why.

The film is the 1944 movie, *The White Cliffs of Dover*.

Not only is this a movie about a boy named John whose father is killed in battle against the Germans during a World War, but because his father's death comes so early in his life, John never gets a chance to know his dad.

Even though it's an extremely veiled reference involving a decades-old movie that few today may even know, there is a clear reason why its appearance is both extremely relevant and potentially soul-jarring to Pink. Roger, whose own father was killed in the war, writes about Pink, whose father was killed in a war, watching a movie about a man whose father was killed in a war; there is an incredible depth there. It is akin to an infinity mirror view of his world; for Pink it is a further blurring of what is real and what isn't.

What is Pink hoping to see? Is this his way of trying to know his father?

In *The White Cliffs of Dover,* when young John grows up, he enlists during the early days of World War II in the same regiment in which his father served. The story does not have a happy ending. Tragically, John also dies as a result of his wounds from combat.

So again, in the same way that Hemingway's Old Man allows himself to suffer as a necessary step in his battle with the fish, Pink tragically allows this deep tumble into his own emotional abyss to happen in order to fortify the defense mechanisms he needs to cope. Given how often Pink's troubled narrative goes back to the void his father's death left behind, there is an obvious nod to mortality.

Day after day, love turns grey like the skin of a dying man.

From the start, the use of decomposition as a metaphor for love's natural decay paints quite a vivid and disturbing picture. Everything dies, including love. But love dies a long, slow death that is sometimes never acknowledged until one partner leaves the other behind.

Night after night, we pretend it's alright.

But I have grown older.

And you have grown colder.
And nothing is very much fun anymore.

These are the "Empty Spaces" between Pink and his wife, the ones that were ignored until it was too late.

And I can feel one of my turns coming on…

Pink admits that he has had these emotional outbursts before. He realizes there is a sleeping monster inside of him — one that he can sense is about to awaken. There is a real "Jekyll and Hyde" relationship going on between Pink and this being that lives inside of his own twisted mirror.

Written by Robert Louis Stevenson and first published in 1886, *The Strange Case of Dr. Jekyll and Mr. Hyde* is an allegoric tale of the duality of being human. Presented as a horror mystery, Stevenson demonstrates how the innocent curiosity about our own darker sides can go out of control to the point that the inner monster takes complete control and destroys one's life. According to Jekyll, the human soul is a battleground between man's inner angels and demons.

I feel cold as a razor blade,
Tight as a tourniquet,

This last lyrical reference shares a duality of its own, since a "tourniquet" is not only something used to stem catastrophic bleeding on a battlefield during times of war, but also, along with "razor blade," serve as indirect references to recreational narcotics. Given the unbridled hedonism we experienced in the circus of flesh during "Young Lust," it's probably safe to assume that wherever sex and rock and roll go, drugs aren't too far behind.

The demons fighting for control inside Pink's mind are many and great.

When you see an iceberg, the portion visible above the waterline is greatly dwarfed by the mass that remains unseen below the surface. Freud also proposed that the Id was very much the same, with most of it hidden from view. According to him, it's not only the libido that sits in the driver's seat of the Id, but also what he referred to as *Thanatos*: the "death instinct," the violent urges of mankind. In Greek mythology, Thanatos is the God of Death. He is the twin brother of Hypnos, the God of Sleep.

"One Of My Turns" is a song that begins in 3/4 time, a meter often associated with waltzes. Pink dances with the truth from behind his wall. Now, in between death and sleep, in a drug-fueled haze, Pink's Id emerges like Mr. Hyde after Dr. Jekyll has downed his doomed potion, and we emerge in 4/4 rock meter.

Run to the bedroom.
In the suitcase on the left
You'll find my favorite axe

This is rife with double meaning. Axe is a modern-day euphemism for an electric guitar or bass. Axes were also the favored weapons of Vikings. Given how hard rockers wielding loud electric guitars as a favored weapon of choice are often wont to compare themselves to modern barbarians it's not hard to see why the term gets thrown around in the world of music. It's probably no coincidence that Gene Simmons of the band Kiss has often played a bass shaped like a large double-bladed battle axe since the 1970s.

Interestingly, the term *axe* is not just a term exclusive to the jargon of rock gods. There is anecdotal evidence of musicians during the pre-war jazz age referring to their saxophones and other instruments as "axes." It is common to hear musicians taking their axe to the "woodshed," in order to practice. This derivative use of the word obviously implies less of a barbarian's usage of the tool than it would a lumberjack's labor and hard work. So here, when Pink refers to his "favorite axe," we definitely feel the implication of his darker (and possibly psychotic) impulses lurking below the surface. In *The Strange Case of Dr. Jekyll and Mr. Hyde*, the monster tramples a young girl. Pink, now unable to control himself, begins to take out his life's frustrations on the poor groupie and his hotel room.

Inside this song, in which duality has such a heavy thematic presence, Waters constructed a wonderful relationship between the dialogue spoken by the groupie before the music starts and the lyrics sung by Pink as his inner demons take control.

...in the suitcase on the left, you'll find my favorite axe? (Are all these your guitars?)

...This is just a passing phase, one of my bad days (Are you feeling okay?)

...Would you like to watch T.V.? (What are you watching?)

...Or get between the sheets? (Wanna take a bath?)

...Contemplate the silent freeway (Hello?)

...Or get something to eat? (Can I get a drink of water?)

Far from being an outlet of his inner rage, this monster is less interested in hurting the girl than he is in trying to make some kind of twisted connections. This is more like Pink's desperate cry for help.

Once he breaks the window, we hear the not-so-silent roadway in the street below. We hear traffic rushing by below his window. Metaphorically, he is standing on the ledge.

Would you like to learn to fly?
Would you like to see me try?

Though he is cleverly letting us tread on the thought of self-annihilation, Waters is letting us know that suicide is indeed an option. Even more importantly, he's letting us know that Pink is not choosing suicide as the answer; he is instead seemingly inviting the groupie to shoot up with him. He is trying to invite her to join him behind his wall.

Why are you running away?

We are hearing his voice fade away, not so much the aural effect of her literally distancing herself from him, but more the sound of him falling ever deeper into the abyss of despair. Now we see that his question is not only directed to the runaway groupie fleeing for her safety, but also directed towards the wife he has lost. The anguish at the tail end of the note's delivery illuminates the true recipient of Pink's sentiment.

*****

DON'T LEAVE ME NOW

"Don't Leave Me Now" begins with guitars pinging like the sonar of ships lost at sea. These haunting echoes of Pink's despair bounce off the walls around him. His labored, heavy breathing takes us deep into disturbed dreams once again. Inside his mind, the "Stages of Grief" tour continues. Having suffered through Shock and Denial (and a certain amount of Pain and Guilt, as well as Anger), we now arrive at Bargaining.

Ooooh babe, don't leave me now
Don't say it's the end of the road
Remember the flowers I sent.

Notice how he calls her "babe," the same way Mother referred to her boy when she was conveniently putting a spin on the truth of the world. He's begging his wife not to leave him in the same way Mother begged him to stay close to her, all the while trying to convince her — and to some extent, himself — that what they had wasn't all that bad. From Pink's injured Ego comes another defense mechanism: "Undoing," his attempt to take back the hurtful behavior heaped along with another big helping of more denial. His voice, usually calmed by the mask he wears in public, has now become more frantic as the raw nerve endings of his emotional pain lay in waste.

I need you, babe
To put through the shredder
In front of my friends…

Pink has been as emotionally abusive to his wife as he has to himself. The irony cannot be overlooked that her infidelity was discovered after yet another bout of Pink using groupies for self-medication. Though a largely unspoken part of the narrative, Pink's downward spiral has been a steady progression throughout his life as his sanity eroded and the wall he built between himself and the rest of the world went up brick by brick. It's not like he suddenly changed one day into this dark, brooding person. We can only speculate on the mental agonies he had put his wife through during their time together, but one thing is certain: it was her time to say "enough."

The sad truth about his insecurities is that he needs to humiliate her in front of his friends, because that's who he is. He needs an emotional punching bag and because she was the only one he could open up to, she suffered the ill effects of his self-destructive behavior. It's the powerless assuming power over others to feel in control. In effect, he's become a bully.

How could you go?
When you know how I need you to beat to a pulp on a Saturday night.
Ooooh babe, don't leave me now

Given the type of aggression buried deep inside his psyche and the emergence of his own troubled *Mr. Hyde* personality, it's hard to escape the poetic brilliance of implying this violence is real. Pink is speaking in very visceral terms. Remember though, he's dreaming here. It could be his manifestation of how angry he is at her considering that the lyrics become very passive/ aggressive.

It is more likely this violent sentiment is used to describe his extreme mental abuse foisted upon her on a regular basis. These particular lyrics very powerful demonstrate what can only be seen as a love/hate relationship with the song's subject. Notice how the words "need you" echo seven times here, reinforcing the importance of this thought.

It's one thing to assume that Pink is singing about his wife. However, there are many distinct narrative parallels here with his life's story so far. There can be little doubt of the passive/aggressive relationship Pink had, at least in his mind, with his mother and her controlling ways. There's also the anguish he has felt nearly all of his life from the death of his father and the anger he feels about the loss of this guiding figure. Both of these figures offer a love/hate relationship for Pink's psyche to chew upon. Let's also not forget that the sheer imagery of being "put through a shredder" harkens back to the industrial slaughterhouse of individuality Pink was put through in the guise of schooling.

Though none of these things by themselves merit consideration as the sole subject of this song, their common universality and lifelong effects on Pink as contributing factors to why he built his wall make it seem quite possible that, in the twisted mirror, this song is one that Pink sings to himself.

In fact, it can be reasonably argued that the subject of this song is *Pink's own sanity.*

How can you treat me this way?

Running away?

So devastating is this final back-breaking blow of wifely betrayal that it has completely fractured Pink's psyche in two. Pink's relationship to reality is severed and he drifts away like an astronaut who has lost the tether between himself and his capsule.

Ground control to Major Pink…

From a musical production standpoint, there is a wonderful audio metaphor playing out in "Don't Leave Me Now" in the form of the "spaceman" echo on the guitar. As opposed to the heavy breathing of sleep, this could be interpreted as the measured breathing inside of a pressurized spacesuit. Because *The Wall* is such a layered work, it could very well be that the nightmare playing inside Pink's troubled sleep is an astronaut drifting away from gravity's embrace into the frigid unknown darkness of space..

Interestingly enough, modern dream analysis involving a "drifting away" scenario implies that the subject feels they have completely lost all control over his or her life.

While both shattered halves of Pink's psyche have chosen flight over fight, they seem to be fleeing in opposite directions. The abusive and self-destructive Id has abandoned the helm and now the much-bruised Ego, left unprotected, reacts like a helpless child. What began as an over-arching fixation on the emptiness of his life now becomes the defense mechanism of regression. Fixation and regression, according to Freud, are definitely formative elements for neurosis. Rather than dealing with impulses in an adult way, regression leads to a reversion of the Ego into an earlier developmental state. In this particular case, Pink's regression is a relapse into infantilism.

By hiding behind this wall of his own creation, he's essentially crawling back into a womb-like state.

This is obviously a very selfish act on Pink's part. Looking at his expressed behavior, though, it is exactly his own selfishness and unwillingness to accept blame for his own actions that has caused this situation.

Why are you running away?

"Don't Leave Me Now" shares a final lyric with "One of My Turns." In the narrative of Pink's life, these two songs are twisted mirror images of each other: cause and effect. Because this insecurity is blamed on his upbringing it causes him, in turn, to be a terrible person to others, causing them to flee, causing him to feel more insecure and alone.

Like an astronaut drifting away.

Beginning at about 3:01, the Hammond organ begins to rumble like a spaceship leaving its launch pad as Gilmour's soulfully sad guitar solo of long sustained notes hangs above us like stars in the sky. Just underneath the solo you have the piano playing arpeggiated chords; the single descending notes evoke a feeling of sinking deeper and deeper into a swirling abyss.

It should be noted that "Don't Leave Me Now" is another song played in 12/8, much like "In the Flesh?" and "The Thin Ice". By taking us back to the same meter as the beginning of *The Wall*, we are coming full circle — not only to Pink's own beginnings (and in the case of "The Thin Ice," his infancy) but also to the cyclical nature of this type of insanity, which threatens to destroy Pink's mind once and for all.

* * * * *

ANOTHER BRICK IN THE WALL
(PART 3)

As the last notes of Gilmour's solo from "Don't Leave Me Now" ring out, hanging in the air like a fading beacon, we hear the unmistakable sound of several television sets switching on. Emotionally spent, Pink retreats to the flickering images on the screens before him. The TV is a mystical device that somehow brings Pink closer to his father; the actors playing soldiers in old war movies have become surrogates for a person Pink never knew.

The old man's ghost is nowhere to be seen. Instead, Pink finds commercials, sports, and talking heads. It all has no substance, which is the same doomed fate he sees for himself, forever playing the unfulfilling role of a rock star without a soul to cling to.

Like Ebenezer Scrooge's Ghost of Christmas Present, Pink's own monsters have given him a horrifying glimpse at the unchecked effect of his actions. Here he sits, alone and unprotected from the world. What Pink sees about himself, he doesn't like.

But no longer will these voices on the TV mock him, nor will the ghost of his father haunt him. As we begin "Another Brick In The Wall (Part 3)," the televisions are now smashed into silence, one by one.

Pink's final connection to the world, his one-way electronic tether, is now removed from his life — its doorway into his world shattered and rendered shut.

I don't need no arms around me.

And I don't need no drugs to calm me.

Again, as with "Another Brick In The Wall (Part 2)," you have the intentional use of the double negative. Literally speaking, he is telling us he *does* need those arms around him. It's a dishonest statement and the tragic irony is that the only one he is lying to is himself. The use of the double negative, perhaps a sign of regression to immaturity, belies his rejection of intimacy. Cleverly layered in the twisted mirror dichotomy of *The Wall* is a duality which implies that not only are these arms around him a form of embrace, but they are also a restraint holding him back. The very drugs which calm him and allow him to function around others prevent him from fulfilling his neurotic desire to complete this self-destructive task he's hell bent upon.

I have seen the writing on the wall.

Don't think I need anything at all...

Pink rationalizes his choice by believing that if he doesn't isolate himself, things will get even worse. His whole universe is going to hell around him. The world could end if they drop the bomb. This is a pattern of doom that he has finally deciphered and for which he finally understands the consequences.

This signals the return of a similar single-note picked "Morse code" motif on guitar that we've heard telegraphed to us in "Another Brick in the Wall (Part 1)" and the industrialized four-on-the-floor beat and tempo of "Another Brick in the Wall (Part 2)," tying these three parts together. As the guitar chords hit, they ring out like the tolling of bells. The synth loop that appears here in the mix gives out a klaxon call.

All in all it was all just bricks in the wall…
All in all YOU were all just bricks in the wall…

This is Pink's blanket condemnation of the world. There is no individual blame-pointing anymore. To him, *everyone* equally caused this pain. It is a defense mechanism born of his own rejection by a world that he believes doesn't understand him. Blame, especially for Pink, is truly a state of denial. Finally convinced that there is no longer any room in his life for wearing the disguise first mentioned during "In The Flesh?" he decides the only safe thing to do is live inside this isolation of his own making. As such, Pink chooses to affix the final bricks into place and completely separate himself from reality for good.

※※※※

GOODBYE CRUEL WORLD

It was 17th century poet John Donne who famously wrote of the metaphysical relationship between man and isolation.

No man is an island
Entire of itself, every man is a piece of the continent

But now, in "Goodbye Cruel World," Pink has chosen to emancipate himself from the rest of us.

From the waning fadeout of the schizophrenic synthesizer loop, a bass emerges playing octave jump quarter notes over a quasi-religious sounding muted organ that enters the mix after the soft tolling of a bell. That octave jump, similar to the first two notes in the melody to "Somewhere Over the Rainbow" is less a veiled clue to the veracity of *Dark Side of the Moon* being created specifically to sync with the movie *The Wizard of Oz* than it is a marker for the slow passing of time in this solemn moment.

But whereas Judy Garland's famous lament was sung back on the farm in Kansas moments before the tornado spun her off to a fantastical world full of danger and wonder, there is a much darker and sinister journey in store for Pink.

Delivered in this brief song is Pink's metaphoric suicide note. Here he is, no longer able to bear the weight of his world, catatonic as he cements the last bricks into his wall.

Goodbye all you people
There's nothing you can say
To make me change my mind
Goodbye…

Again, the blame comes as a blanket statement. *You people* who drove him to this choice, this is your fault. He is tired of fighting with you on your terms.

There is none of the anguish in Pink's voice previously heard when he asks, "Why are you running away?" Instead, there is only a very serene Pink, who has embraced acceptance of his assigned fate. Like a monk making a solemn journey to his penance, he marches forward with his decision under the bass line's metaphoric tolling of bells. In their own duality, not only does this tolling serve as a herald of Pink's final move to isolation, but also as a harbinger of the darkness yet ahead on the path.

Donne's poem finishes with the eponymous line:
For whom the bell tolls;
It tolls for thee.

What Donne refers to is actually a funeral bell, one whose tolling marks not only the loss of one individual, but a loss for all.

As the last brick falls into place, Pink is effectively silenced and now what stands between Pink and all of reality is *The Wall.* He is destroyed, but not defeated. If so, he would have leapt off that balcony. It is his spirit that is broken and has crawled back into a womb of his own making in order to find salvation and rebirth.

And as we will see in the dramatic second half, from the ashes of disdain Pink will be reborn. However, it is not the phoenix that awaits. Instead it is the steely-eyed crow, set to not only control his new destiny, but that of others under a dark spell of fear.

Let us not forget that *The Wall* is not just the story of one man's self-destruction. It is, in fact, an allegory which speaks to the self-destructive tendencies of isolating oneself from the world and those around you. The thin veneer of fantasy is there only to prop up Pink as a sock puppet stand-in for our own neuroses.

Because let us never forget for whom the bell truly tolls.

✷ ✷ ✷ ✷ ✷

PART TWO

HEY YOU

We rejoin Pink mentally and symbolically imprisoned behind his wall and physically "imprisoned" in his locked hotel room, which now has a broken window that overlooks a busy street. Fully conscious realization over what he has done sets in and "Hey You" is Pink's desperate cry for help.

The second half of *The Wall begins* as an undistorted six-string acoustic guitar rings out notes of pure crystal. This echo-rich guitar floats inside a big space, not inside the claustrophobic confines Pink committed himself to at the end of the first half. This guitar gives us a sense of the infinite. Here, Gilmour is not only picking a minor chord, but one whose added 9th evokes a true air of mystery and foreboding. Considering the troubled journey that has delivered us to this moment, it wouldn't be half crazy to mistake the arpeggiated chords for the iconic riff from *Twilight Zone* played in reverse.

Hey you, out there in the cold, getting lonely, getting old... can you feel me?

Pink has been pulled apart by an internal war between his Id's primal desires and his Ego's reluctance to get hurt. It is now up to the part of his psyche known as the Super-Ego to fix the situation. Freud called the Super-Ego the part of our personality that provides our internal guidelines for making judgments. In short, it is his conscience. Called into action, his conscience now must reconcile Pink's situation through association.

You get the sense that Pink is pleading to be recognized. But it's not so much "Pink" the character in this narrative that begs to be noticed as much as it is "Pink" the metaphor. In cinematic three-act structure, there is an extremely important moment known as "the midpoint." At the midpoint, there should be an event in the protagonist's journey that changes *everything* and alters the trajectory of his path. In this case, the midpoint was triggered by the shattering of Pink's spirit via the discovery of his wife's infidelity and the subsequent crumbling of his psyche like a house of cards in an earthquake.

In "Hey You," Waters gives us an entire song brilliantly rendered as a recap, reinforcing the allegory already presented. In a truly genius move, the first voice — the calm, serene David Gilmour voice – is not only a poetic overview, but also turns the twisted mirror around and speaks directly to *you* the listener (Hey You!) in the same voice.

Hey you, standing in the aisles with itchy feet and fading smiles… can you feel me?

While one may be inclined to believe this line refers to the concert goers who are Pink's fans, I would beg to differ. "Itchy feet and fading smiles" obviously refer to those who are tiring of an act — but at this point in the fictional narrative of Pink's life we have not seen any evidence that his fans have expressed *any* disappointment in Pink. In fact, from the information we've been given — including the voracious sexual appetites of the groupies and the money Pink must still be generating to be holed up in such a grand hotel room — one would think that the fervor of his fans fervor hasn't diminished at all. For them, at least, it's business as usual.

No, I believe that there's a sly double meaning at play here. First, the mention of "aisles" refers to those found at a stage play. In this case it's the performance Pink puts on in his everyday life; those with the itchy feet and fading smiles are people who have grown tired of what they see in him. This is the subliminal message that breaks the fourth wall and talks directly to the listener of this album. Effectively, Waters makes an appeal to those who may not quite understand what is going on in *The Wall*, those who are looking for answers that aren't so abstract, and asks them to be patient and let the narrative play out.

Waters is suggesting that even if you don't get it right now, if you feel *something* from *The Wall* you need to trust that he will eventually lead you to an emotional payoff.

Hey you, don't help them to bury the light.

It's a common metaphor for "the truth." The light that Pink sings about is his soul: that which makes him unique and special. It's a reference to the lobotomization of individuality achieved through the bullying and repressive industrialization lamented in "Another Brick In The Wall (Part 2)." The teachers, and those who wish to control others by curbing undesirable traits of individuality, do not commit their sins against humanity by themselves. By turning a blind eye and allowing it to happen, *we* are accomplices to these crimes.

We've already talked about how a brilliant storyteller knows to reinforce what you've already been shown by recapping it (without being obvious). By dusting the fingerprints of this reference to "the light," there's another layer that plays directly into the central themes of *The Wall.*

The Shining by Stephen King is a horror novel about isolation and insanity. The story takes place at an old hotel named the Overlook, out in the middle of nowhere, closed off from the rest of the world during winter. Lead character Jack Torrance brings his family to this most isolated of locations to take a job as caretaker, also hoping the locale will allow him to finish writing his next book. Jack is an abusive alcoholic; this unwanted legacy inherited from his late father causes Jack's wife Wendy to be distant. Though they know their son Danny has the ability to read minds (second sight!), they cannot even talk about it between themselves.

Danny becomes isolated due to his young age and feeling different because of his "gift." Jack becomes isolated by the process of his writing. Soon the Torrance family spirals into even deeper isolation, not only from the outside world, but from each other. The ghosts haunting the Overlook convince Jack that he should kill his family and join them as permanent guests of the hotel.

The Shining is a novel about how extreme stress and carrying the weight of one's past can greatly impair our ability to deal with reality. However, King shrewdly leaves the story open to interpretation as to whether it was evil spirits or the isolation which caused the insanity.

Were the events "real," or were they just part of a shared psychosis?

Coincidentally, the title of *The Shining* was inspired by John Lennon's song "Instant Karma" from the *Plastic Ono Band* album, the same album which featured Lennon's morose parental ode "Mother." Given *The Shining*'s status as a runaway international bestseller in

1977, it's not without merit to suspect there's at least a trace of influence to be found within the parallels between it and *The Wall*.

There's even an aspect of "burying the light" that wistfully refers back to Syd Barrett. It was his spark of individuality that made him special; that light was dimmed by the drugs that ruined his life and ultimately extinguished forever by his institutionalization.

Light is a powerful metaphor because it works on so many levels.

Another metaphor that works well in "Hey You" is the use of "carry the stone," a very heavy (pun intended) symbol for the lifetime aggregate of emotional weight one bears from their wrongdoings. Floyd fans will instantly recognize "the stone" from its previous appearance in the song "Dogs" from the *Animals* album. In "Dogs," the stone belonging to the evil, greedy man in the song is so heavy that it eventually drowns him. It's almost like something out of Greek mythology.

By drawing from previous works outside *The Wall*, Waters gives a special nod to the faithful and helps add depth to Pink's story and character by planting a flag in the mental real estate he already owns in the mind of the fan.

Taking into account the multi-layered meanings woven into the song, Gilmour's vocal is certainly speaking directly to us, the listener. By asking us to help Pink *carry the stone*, he's inferring that because *The Wall* is not a cookie-cutter, spoon-fed narrative, we are absolutely right to fill in the blanks of this poetic and metaphor-rich story. In short, he's inviting us to think!

In this regard, David Gilmour's voice is not just Pink's consciousness, but our own as well. By telling us *open your heart, I'm coming home* he's not only implying that Pink's Ego no longer wants to be exiled from the rest of his psyche, but also telling the audience to "hang in there, an emotional payoff to this story will be coming."

From the launch pad of the guitar solo comes the growling Hammond organ, evoking the feeling of rumbling rocket engines. Gilmour's deft six-string slinging vaults us into a journey through our own subconscious. The guitar solo also tells us the tale of Pink's life, from this rumble that birthed him (akin to the rumble of a bomb), to the torment of his childhood and rebellion of youth and his school years, as evidenced by the repetition of the iconic four note riff from "Another Brick in the Wall (Part 2)."

Then, in the second half of the solo, Gilmour gets dirty. He takes us through an "I done gone lost my woman" blues feel, ending his cry with a scream. Given that we are in a minor key, it is not a scream of joy.

As Waters takes up the vocals after the solo, we have not only changed singers but also changed character. Here, Waters is not Pink in any form; instead he serves as a sort of Greek chorus, essentially summarizing what is wrong with Pink.

But it was only a fantasy.
The Wall was too high as you can see.
No matter how he tried, he could not break free.
And the worms ate into his brain.

It is all a mental condition. There's no real "wall," so to speak. The irony is that we, the audience, already know this (or are supposed to know this by now). But as album narratives are often consumed in a non-linear fashion, the quick recap places Pink's self-imposed condition into perspective for those joining the story "in progress" (or those who perhaps haven't been paying close attention to the lyrics so far).

Underneath the Greek chorus, down in the mix, there is a synthesizer sound: an electronic brass playing triumphant major chord horns as if to proclaim the truth. But then, from the small crescendo on the word 'brain' comes another, less positive-minded synth sound. This one, like the buzzing of insects inside Pink's mind, is the static that prevents him from clear and rational thought.

Again we hear the crystal clear guitars playing that reverse *Twilight-Zone*-riff arpeggio. This time it is joined by the sliding notes of a fretless bass. The bass guitar often implies the chordal and modal direction of a song by the progression of notes it plays; sometimes holding down a chord's root in the background and playing a passing tone to smoothly reach the next change. In this regard, it serves as the subconscious of a song. Here, by emerging for a moment in this solo, the bass is reminding us of the role the subconscious plays in the decisions being made.

As we come to the third and final verse of "Hey You," we are presented with yet *another* voice. Also sung by Waters, this persona is much more frantic. This panicked voice is the embodiment of Pink's subconscious. It is what little is left of the rational part of Pink's psyche and it sounds desperate because it *is* desperate.

By addressing the one who is "out there on the road, always doing what you're told," the Super-Ego is speaking directly to that part of Pink that has become numbed by the way his rock star existence has turned him into a commodity with no control over his life. When he calls out to the one "out there beyond the wall, breaking bottles in the hall," he addresses the rebellious and angry Pink who exhibits these signs of being mentally unhinged. He's pleading with himself not to let the bastards win. He's begging Pink not to throw in the towel.

Hey you, don't tell me there's no hope at all...

Without detente, Pink risks the same fate as his father. Though the specific war that threatens to claim Pink as a victim is one being waged inside him, it is no less deadly. The metaphoric worms that feast on the buried flesh of the dead now eat into Pink's brain. The frenetic madness his voice takes on as the song progresses is a testament to the decay of insanity that has infected his rational thought.

By having Pink's Super-Ego address his tormented Id, a dynamic is created that lets the lyrics speak to everyone in the world suffering from something similar. This gives us a sense that we share the same problems as Pink. Waters delivers a very powerful message by talking not only to himself, but to those like him.

The walking wounded.

Once more, this is a case of "For Whom the Bell Tolls" and giving the listener a subliminal nod that it indeed *Tolls For Thee.*

Interestingly enough, as Waters uses all of this pleading of Pink's Super-Ego for the rest of his psyche to "get the band back together," so to speak, he is also making a bold statement about the unity of humankind; *Together we stand. Divided we fall* ties into the central theme of *The Wall* as well as Donne's famous poem.

No man is an island
Entire of itself, every man is a piece of the continent

Sadly though, a happy reconciliation is not to be had. The echoed repetition of the lyric "we fall" emphasizes that as Pink refuses the outstretched hand of his Super-Ego, he slips deeper and deeper into oblivion's wake.

✳ ✳ ✳ ✳

IS THERE ANYBODY OUT THERE ?

Is there anybody out there?

David Gilmour makes a wonderful atmospheric seagull noise with his guitar. Far from being a synthesized or electronic-based sound, it's instead a simple, lo-tech sonic creation made by plugging a guitar into the output jack of a wah-wah pedal and then taking the output from the device's input jack. Crank up your amp, add a little delay and, by controlling this self-oscillating feedback tone with the volume and tone knobs, you get a noise reminiscent of a seagull crying or laughing.

Probably the most famous appearance of the Pink Floyd gull sound is from the middle section of the band's twenty-three and a half minute long opus "Echoes," the extended finale of their 1971 album *Meddle.* "Echoes" reflects Roger Waters shift from writing about space travel and psychedelia to a more focused look at the issues facing humanity — specifically those which deal with perceptions in our own minds. Though most of "Echoes" is instrumental, lyrically it's about the ability to identify with others and understanding the human relationship we all have with each other.

In other words, no man is an island.

The way he portrays this narrative makes it a very intimate struggle. Psychologically, the solitary seagull sound lends itself to an interpretation of loneliness. Close your eyes; you can just imagine standing by yourself, staring out at a vast sea with only this bird to call your name.

Though the conceptual imagery of a seagull may have lost some of its symbolic meaning since "Echoes" first came out, it should not be forgotten that, at the time, Richard Bach's 1970 novella *Jonathan Livingston Seagull* was a blockbuster global literary sensation. The story is essentially a fable about a bird that becomes disillusioned and frustrated being told how to act and live. Unable to conform, he becomes an exile from the flock. During the 1970's, there was a much more omnipresent pop-culture shorthand associated with the seagull in terms of isolation and the mythical (and mostly trying) search for self.

In the same way that some people believe that *Dark Side of the Moon* can be synchronized with *The Wizard of Oz*, there is a school of belief that "Echoes" syncs up with the final segment of Stanley Kubrick's 1968 sci-fi masterpiece *2001: A Space Odyssey*, a movie not only about space exploration and the perils of technology, but also the future of humanity. In the movie's final segment, titled "Jupiter and Beyond the Infinite," astronaut Dr. David Bowman is pulled, alone, into a star gate tunnel of colored light; there he is granted an understanding of the meaning of existence before he himself transcends from his human form into an energy that is one with the universe, ensuring, as such, that he will never be alone.

So it's not unreasonable to suggest that, within the scope of this unique and simple seagull noise, a deep sense of *existentialism* is implied.

A very deep layer is added to the narrative in "Is There Anybody Out There?" by drawing on a Pink Floyd fan's recognition (consciously or not) of this sound from "Echoes." Granted it is quite a long way to travel to make this point; however, it's hard to deny that when Gilmour evokes the gull noise, we are effectively reminded of the lonely and haunting struggle of trying to discover the true meaning of life.

As the song begins, through the broken hotel room window, we can hear the traffic below. Vehicles pass by, carrying people to their destinations, oblivious to the struggle playing out in the mind of a rock star above. Once more the television switches on; this time the episode "Fandango" from the old western TV series *Gunsmoke* plays.

Marshall Dillon: "Well, only about an hour of daylight left. We better get started."

Miss Tyson: "Is it unsafe to travel at night?"

Marshall Dillon: "It'll be a lot less safe to stay here. Your father's gonna pick up our trail before long."

As Pink sits alone in his hotel room, behind the wall of his own creation, he hides from the ghosts in his mind, including that of the deceased father whose absence has haunted him his entire life.

Fading into the mix is the ominous drone of a synthesizer playing a low C. Soon the buzzing of the "bugs" inside his brain return to amplify our understanding of the madness that eats at him.

Is there anybody out there?

Though this question, asked four times with varying inflection, makes up the sum total of the lyrics in this song, it is far from a minimalist exercise in portraying Pink's isolation. Pink finally realizes what he's done. Now he calls for help from the other side of the wall. It is an S.O.S.

But there is no reply.

True to form in *The Wall*'s twisted mirror dichotomy, "Is There Anybody Out There?" is a song that swings on a hinge right at a midpoint. Listen as the bass notes play a descending scale; if you hold to the ideal that the bass is the subconscious of a song, you can read into this segue as Pink's continuing descent. But here it's peaceful. The rumble of the TV and the rushing traffic below his broken window fade away into this pastoral dream-like state. An instrumental interlude played by a nylon string classical guitar and a several orchestral instruments emerges from this foreboding emptiness and fear of being alone.

The guitar's simple arpeggiated figures, played in A minor, sound suspended and moody; a violin's high notes insert an essence of pathos, but it is the woodwinds, primarily the oboe, that portray a certain pastoral sensibility.

Pink has now entered the first stage of the butterfly transformation that occurs during the second half of *The Wall*.

This classically oriented interlude was not Waters' idea, but that of producer Bob Ezrin, who wanted to flesh out the connective tissue of this transformation between "Is There Anybody Out There?" and "Nobody Home." Recorded and arranged by film composer Michael Kamen, the interlude doesn't even include any members from the actual band. The nylon-string acoustic guitar was not played by David Gilmour, but instead by Ron DiBiasi, a session guitarist hired by Kamen. Nonetheless, it is an effective and emotionally worthy companion, much like the other creative contributions Ezrin made by adding the children's chorus to "Another Brick In The Wall (Part 2)." It fits seamlessly into the overall narrative of *The Wall* by heightening the emotions we share with Pink.

This serenity Pink has found inside his world only lasts a short while; once again the traffic and TV set fade back in. There's only so long he can keep from noticing the walls around him and the memories that scar him.

And the fact that he is totally alone.

*****

NOBODY HOME

There is a somewhat well-known Pink Floyd anecdote about how Syd Barrett showed up to the studio at Abbey Road one day, seven years after he had been pushed out of the band. He was overweight, with shaved head and eyebrows.(hey, remember that from the movie?), clutching a plastic bag containing a toothbrush and other toiletries. Ironically, the band was completing the final mix of "Shine On You Crazy Diamond," which, of course, is completely about Syd. In a later interview, Richard Wright recalled the jarring event, mentioning that both he and Roger were reduced to tears.

According to Wright, there was something in Syd's eyes – or, more appropriately, *nothing* in them.

There was nobody home.

More than just the answer to the question posed in the previous song, "Nobody Home" contains an abundance of feeling and history surrounding the band. As such, it's possibly the most autobiographic song on the album. Written by Waters during the end of *The Wall* recording sessions, "Nobody Home" features Bob Ezrin on the piano, mostly due to the further fracturing of the band by the official ousting of Richard Wright as a member of Pink Floyd. One cannot help but feel

Waters' disdain for Wright in the lyrics that describe his now-former band mate.

I got nicotine stains on my fingers
I got a silver spoon on a chain
Got a grand piano to prop up my mortal remains

In truth, though, this song is most heavily influenced by the lingering presence of the ghost of Syd Barrett.

I've got a little black book with my poems in.
Got a bag with a toothbrush and a comb in.
When I'm a good dog they sometimes throw me a bone in.

It's not just a statement about the lack of control Pink has over his life, or that he's treated like a "good dog" who is rewarded when done what he's told. Instead, Pink is effectively committing an act of self-actualization by taking inventory of his life. It's a very optimistic thing to do in a way.

However, the end result takes a rather depressing turn when he realizes he has been reduced to a mere set of basic possessions. When he speaks of the elastic bands that keep his shoes on, one may think he's referring to the tattered footwear of a disheveled man with rubber bands keeping them from falling apart — perhaps like Syd, standing there overweight, out of sorts and clutching his bag of toiletries.

Cleverly, this particular line holds a dual sense of imagery with the Gohil's boots that are name-checked later on in the song. Gohil's is a shoe store in Camden, North London. In the late 1960's, short ankle boots with an elasticated "gusset" (rather than laces) were "de rigeur" with the musical in-crowd and Gohil's was *the* place to get them.

There's even photographic evidence that conclusively ties Syd to this very reference.

In mid-1968, after his departure (or what some would say, ouster) from the band, Syd returned to London to begin recording a solo album. To say things did not go smoothly would be a vast understatement. Following a breakup with his girlfriend, Syd abruptly stopped recording after only a few months of work with former Floyd manager Peter Jenner producing. Syd took off on a solo drive around Britain to clear his head and eventually ended up in a psychiatric ward in Cambridge. Though production would pick up again in 1969 with a much-rested Syd, it would still prove to be a difficult project that eventually required the help of former band mates Roger Waters and David Gilmour to finish. The resulting album, *The Madcap Laughs,* would see the light of day in January of 1970. It was during the photo sessions for the album cover, with Mick "The Man Who Shot the 70's" Rock, that a picture was taken of Syd clearly wearing a pair of Gohil's. This shot would later be published in a now out-of-print book of rock star photographs by Mick "The Man Who Shot the 70s" Rock.

Evoking Syd Barrett, from this point on "Nobody Home" gives more definitive evidence of narcotics in Pink's life in the form of "swollen hand blues." This is a reference to heroin. Users who inject themselves in their hands damage their veins, often impairing their blood circulation. As a result, their hands swell.

What of the tragedy of having *13 channels of shit on the TV to choose from?* Sadly, Pink is surrounded by a wall of faces from the glowing box, but he cannot make a connection with any of them.

I've got electric light.

And I've got second sight.

"Second sight" is a term often used to describe psychic ability, such as being able to read minds like young Danny Torrance from *The Shining.* As it did with Danny, this incredible difference between himself and others has isolated Pink. The electric light is a metaphor of mental illumination, such as the kind portrayed for comic effect when a light bulb appears over some character's head. When it pops on, it indicates an idea has come to light; given the paranoia festering inside Pink's mind, there are indeed many ideas turning on.

With that in mind, an interesting thing happens musically right here. Up until this point, there is only piano and voice. But at the beginning of *I've got electric light,* a single violin comes in holding the note of C. This then jumps a perfect 5th up to a G at the start of *And I've got second sight* before finally resolving up a 4th to a C, one octave higher than where it started. Far from just following the chord progression in the song, there's a real significance to this simple three note string part. To get a better understanding, we're going to have to look at composer Richard Strauss' epic *Also Sprach Zarathustra,* better known as the main theme from the movie *2001: A Space Odyssey.*

The central melody to *Zarathustra* is made up of the same sequence of three notes. The C rises up a 5th to G, then up a 4th to C, an octave up from where we started. In western music (and, generally, in all pop music), the core relationship is made up of these two intervals, the perfect 5th and the perfect 4th ; there is a certain strength portrayed when those intervals are played together. The reason our human ears respond so favorably to them is essentially a function of physics. Play three notes composed of those intervals and then hold them — their overlapping frequencies actually feedback on themselves, reinforcing the original notes in a way that our hearing finds very positive and strong.

In addition to *2001: A Space Odyssey*, there are signature appearances of this particular series of ascending intervals in such iconic cinema as John William's themes for *Star Wars* and *Superman,* as well as Jerry Goldsmith's often overlooked theme for the original *Star Trek: The Motion Picture.* Played together, what these notes evoke in the mind is symbolic— not only of heroism and exploration, but also transcendence.

I've got amazing powers of observation.

Pink is transcending from his original state. He's describing psychic and observational abilities that evoke a sense of omnipotence.

And that's how I know
When I try to get through
On the telephone to you
There will be nobody home...

If there's any doubt to Pink's implied sense of heroism, listen to how triumphant the horns sound behind these four lines. Pink's delusions (and the cult of his celebrity and fame) have made him believe he is a modern Christ-like, even God-like figure (Let there be electric light!).

Let us not forget the spitting incident that became the catalyst for *The Wall*. Roger, feeling above the audience — not only physically from the stage, but also spiritually — momentarily allowed his own delusions of grandeur to turn into a God complex. Because of this well-known bit of Floyd history and the blurring of the lines between Pink's and Roger's lives, you get a real sense that these lyrics also relate closely to his fear that the audience will not get what he's trying to say artistically, especially from underneath the electric lights of the stage.

As to what is exacerbating these delusions, the further implication, once again, is drugs.

The Hendrix perm also alludes to Syd Barrett who, like many rockers of that early 70's era, wore that hairstyle. Pinhole burns is an obvious narcotics reference. In one interview, Waters described that white satin shirt as being his and the pinhole burns coming as a result of smoking hash.

I got nicotine stains on my fingers
I got a silver spoon on a chain
Got a grand piano to prop up my mortal remains.

According to Waters this indeed is a direct reference to Richard Wright. The silver spoon on a chain was a favorite fad accoutrement of the time for heavy users of cocaine. Destructive drugs can certainly cause behaviors like "wild staring eyes" and "a strong urge to fly."

Here again, a reference to flight. This reinforces that the previous mention in "One of My Turns" doesn't refer to jumping to one's death from the hotel room, but instead to feeling like a caged bird that wants to stretch his wings away from the flock and be somebody/something else. Pink, however, like many of us, is unable to achieve this due to the restraints, restrictions and walls that our lives and ourselves have placed in the way.

No matter what he does, Pink cannot connect with others in his life, especially the wife who is never there to get his calls.

What's amazing about Pink taking this inventory of his life is there are no possessions that tie him to his past. There is no photo of his mother or talisman of his father. Instead, Pink has only the life of a rock star who lives out of a suitcase in fancy hotels that all look the same, the malaise one feels on the road for endless months at a time, and how that life destroys your soul.

The lack of belongings that tie him to the past seems to be metaphorical of the disjoint Pink/Roger feels from his audience. Those faded roots are perhaps not a nod toward aging, but instead an acknowledgement that the hedonistic big rock star is no longer the person he once used to be.

Though Pink has that electric light — surprise, surprise, surprise…

There's nobody home.

* * * * *

VERA

Does anybody here remember Vera Lynn?

What seemingly begins as a lament over someone who has gone turns into the abandonment of hope over a vanished promise finally let go.

You're probably asking "just who is this Vera Lynn anyway?"

"Vera" begins with a return to Pink's TV set, now playing a clip from the 1969 World War II movie *The Battle of Britain*. The actual Battle of Britain, waged in 1940, was a campaign by the German Luftwaffe to gain superiority over the R.A.F. and British airspace. It was also the longest sustained bombing assault of the war to that date. At the beginning of World War II, Roger's father, Eric had been a conscientious objector. It was after driving an ambulance during the sustained bombing of London during The Blitz that Eric Fletcher Waters changed his mind and enlisted as a soldier.

Only to go off and die in battle.

In the *Battle of Britain* movie clip, we hear someone yell out "Where the hell are you? Where the hell are you, Simon?" followed by fighter plane caliber machine gun fire, an engine whining from damage and, finally, a crash and explosion as a pilot meets his doom.

Once again the element of flying, a method of departure, is interjected into the narrative. Because the only way Pink can know his dad is through these avatars he sees in old war movies, we are again thematically hitting an important part of the story arc dealing with his father's ghost.

Vera Lynn is not someone we've been introduced to before. She's not someone who Pink/Roger knows in person, nor is she a mosaic of people from his past like the schoolteacher. Instead, she was an extremely popular female singer in the U.K. during World War II. In 1939, U.K. Newspaper the *Daily Express* asked servicemen to name their favorite singers; Vera Lynn was the number one choice. This led to her becoming referred to as "The (Armed) Forces Sweetheart." She is best known for singing the songs "There'll Always Be an England" and another little ditty called "We'll Meet Again."

We'll meet again.

Don't know where. Don't know when.

But I know we'll meet again, some sunny day.

Because of how deeply it resonated with troops going off to war and with their families, "We'll Meet Again" became one of the most famous songs of the era. It was cherished because the optimism of the assertion "we'll meet again" was so enthusiastically, perhaps desperately, embraced; many soldiers didn't survive the war and this song, about how our relationships with other people never end even after they (or we) die, gave folks a link to those who would never come home. Because this meeting place at some time in the future was interpreted by many as being heaven, there was a great comfort in the message.

In 1941, the year of The Blitz, Vera Lynn would launch her own radio show which, besides being broadcast across the country, was played for troops serving abroad. Using her status as a morale booster during the darkest days of the war, she would visit hospitals and perform songs requested by her many soldier listeners. In 1942, she re-recorded "We'll Meet Again" and a year later would star in a war movie of the same name. There is little doubt that Vera Lynn was one of the most beloved entertainers of her time.

All because her music delivered a message that really spoke to people.

Vera! Vera!
What has become of you?
Does anybody else in here feel the way I do?

There's no hiding the disillusioned tone in this last question. This is Pink/Roger's way of telling us that he doesn't believe in Vera's optimistic message any longer. The use of her music and popularity as a tool for propaganda to get people to feel better about going to war no longer sits well with him. Essentially, he's asking if anyone remembers how she told us a little white lie to get us to comply.

Most of the boys who went off to war and died probably had very little choice in how their lives would play out. However, there's a real sense in "We'll Meet Again" of viewing the fear of dying in war through a pair of rose-colored glasses, and the prospect of some kind of cheerful reunion, even if you die, no longer holds sway over Pink/Roger.

To Pink, the realization that this is an empty promise is an epiphany akin to the realization that "Mother" told him everything would be alright not because it would be, but to protect him from the pants-shitting reality that the world is an unforgiving and merciless place. He's asking, "Hey, remember Vera? Remember what she did?", and by doing so is inciting us into viewing Vera Lynn as a puppet of the regime. In this menagerie of Pink's mind, he now feels betrayed, lied to, and manipulated by the same kind of authoritarian forces that took his own daddy away.

As an artist, most of the time you can't just come out and say what you mean because there are too many people who misinterpret a literal translation and twist it to fit their own propaganda. For Roger to come out and say "Vera Lynn lied" or even "Vera Lynn was used by the government to perpetuate a lie in order to soothe the anguish of knowing some of those boys wouldn't come back home alive" would be inflammatory.

Instead, he says it in his own veiled way.

Musically, this song is a lament. Vera Lynn is not a villain. As a massively popular entertainer, touring the country and the world, her existence must have in some ways mirrored Pink's own. She was a superstar. Asking if we even remember her, given the scope of her enormous popularity just a generation before Pink's, is a real statement about the impermanence of fame and myth of pop stardom immortality. If we don't remember her, how can we possibly remember Pink? The dual-edged sword here is that asking what became of her also begs the question of "how did she cope without the fame?"

Furthermore, it helps foreshadow the narrative. If the words of the lovely Vera Lynn can help the war machine generate the cannon fodder needed to (hopefully) achieve victory, then just imagine the extreme power of suggestion that a cult of personality can generate.

By calling her out, Pink/Roger not only declares that he no longer holds onto the link to his father, but also that the death and pain of war is not made any nobler by the abstract ideal of liberty within the rule of an authoritarian force. War is still horrific.

*****

BRING THE BOYS BACK HOME

Magnificent in in its grandeur and very operatic in nature, "Bring the Boys Back Home" sounds like it was lifted right out of *Les Miserables,* a musical which involves a bitter man who finally finds redemption. However, narratively within the layers of this classically oriented song, there is much more going on than the spark of a revolution.

Roger Waters has stated on several occasions that that "Bring the Boys Back Home" is the most important song on *The Wall.* The first time I heard that, I was admittedly a bit surprised. Now I understand the sentiment.

Don't leave the children on their own, no, no...

In the overall context of the autobiographical events that intertwine the real life Roger Waters and the fictional Pink, the implication is that we are doing irreparable harm to future generations by taking away their fathers and mothers.

However, what originally eluded me was how it all really fit into the context of the narrative. Both "Vera" and "Bring the Boys Back Home" are short and don't really have the same moodiness as the rest of side two. But like *The Wall* itself, a story told in two distinct halves, "Vera/Bring the Boys Back Home" form a twisted mirror relationship with each other. They also share an auditory umbilical cord in the musical segue that connects them – "Vera," though in the key of G, ends on a big C chord, the very same key as "Bring the Boys Back Home."

In the first half ("Vera"), Waters illustrates that where war is concerned, governments lie to you and don't value your life or your family's future. You are just a commodity that will be conditioned as a mindless drone to accept their demands and obey their orders. They used the celebrity of Vera Lynn to send the message: "Hey, go off to war. It'll be okay…" To Roger's eyes, this is indeed a problem, one that requires the mindful artist to shed light on in order for the truth to be recognized by others.

In the second half ("Bring the Boys Back Home"), his solution is to say what Vera Lynn could not.

Sure, extolling such a message and taking advantage of the bully pulpit and the spotlight to go off-message probably would have equaled career suicide for Vera Lynn. Yet, this is exactly the white-knuckle fear Waters expresses as a metaphor in how he has built these two songs and dovetailed them together with such emotional clarity. Much as speaking out against the war would have been a huge risk for Vera Lynn, producing *The Wall* was a huge risk for Pink Floyd, both creatively and fiscally. Given the band's precarious financial situation, had *The Wall* bombed (no pun intended), it would have meant ruin for Pink Floyd.

In this case, the risk paid off. It is only because Waters twisted this self-referential mirror upon himself and his first-hand experience (albeit mostly veiled) of the effects of war even beyond the battlefield — and the destructive ripples it causes in the lives left behind — that he is able to make his point here by speaking his message directly to us in plain English.

Bring the boys back home.

In the same way that the narrative of *The Wall* is full of balance between examples of cause and effect, Roger repeats this message knowing that it is one thing for him, in the guise of Pink, to say it, but it becomes much more powerful when *the listener* says it, then asks "how can it be made possible?"

The only answer is quite simple: End war.

There is no doubt of the war being waged inside Pink's psyche for control of his mind. The idea of these battles against his demons is enhanced by the sonic imagery utilized by the fade in of the military-style snare drum rat-a-tatting in the same 12/8 time signature that opens the pomp and circumstance of "In The Flesh?" The instrumentation is totally orchestral, complete with choir echoing the lyrics sung by a frantic Pink. With Michael Kamen weaving in John Phillips Souza-esque piccolo and string flourishes, which are shrouded in more patriotic symbolism than a flag draped coffin, the duality of the song's militaristic musical arrangement emphasizes the purely pacifist message of "Bring the Boys Back Home."

It is the use of this patriotic pastiche that underscores the absurdity of believing such wartime songs as "We'll Meet Again" have any real ability to comfort the intense loss of loved ones who die in battle. By deftly shoving this patriotic musical motif in our faces, he's not only calling out Vera Lynn but also trying to subconsciously alter the way we recognize how such music can be used as pro-war propaganda.

Johnny, get your gun, get your gun, get your gun.
Take it on the run, on the run, on the run.
Hear them calling you and me,
Every Son of Liberty.
Hurry right away, no delay, go today.
Make your Daddy glad to have had such a lad.

Tell your sweetheart not to pine,
To be proud her boy's in line.

These are the lyrics to the first verse of the classic war song "Over There," the American musical counterpart to "We'll Meet Again." In terms of treading upon the mental and emotional real estate owned by pro-war music then planting a flag of pacifism to great commercial and artistic success, Waters is not alone.

In 1939, author and screenwriter Dalton Trumbo unveiled his anti-war masterpiece *Johnny Got His Gun.* An obvious twisted-mirror play on the lyrics made famous in "Over There," the novel *Johnny Got His Gun* was a terrifying story about Joe Bonham, a soldier serving in World War I who goes off to battle and is horrifically injured by an exploding artillery shell. As Joe later awakes in a hospital bed, he can't understand why he is unable to communicate with anyone. It is only after the realization that he has lost not only both his arms and legs, but also his eyes, ears and tongue that he becomes aware that he is now a prisoner trapped inside of a body that refuses to die. Within the confines of Joe's mind, there is not only the tragic recollection of a family and girlfriend he will never see or speak to again that haunt his endless hours of agony, but like a hell unto itself, he experiences tormented thoughts on the myths and realities of war.

Key to the central themes of *Johnny Got His Gun* is the very unequal bargain of war. It is only at the cost of such an unspeakable injury that Joe Bonham realizes that while most men go off to war for idealist hopes, the goals of war have almost nothing to do with men of lower or middle classes; common people like himself have absolutely nothing to gain by fighting wars dictated by the terms of others. The abstract idea that there is something noble in war does not detract from the terrible fact that it offers little to no comfort to those who suffer its pain and death; instead, it only further spreads seeds of isolation born of suffering.

The overall concept of ending global hostilities is the least ambiguous message in *The Wall*'s narrative. There is also an appeal made to those survivors of the internal mental struggles of loved ones. Those who have wandered out alone, lost in the fog of their own emotional difficulties or trapped behind the walls of their creation, need help. Sometimes, just lighting a beacon to illuminate the path is not enough. Sometimes, we have to make an effort to go out and bring those boys and girls back home where they belong.

Unfortunately for Pink, even this inspirational moment in his mind, where he finds a way toward his own redemption via an epiphany to be shared from the spotlight he occupies, is swallowed by the fog of his own insanity. Underscoring the difficulty of his struggles, the voices of these ghosts from his past and the sound of insane laughter drive him to burrow deeper into his cocoon. It is his cry, "Is there anybody out there?" that leads him to fear that nobody will hear him no matter how important his message may be.

✳ ✳ ✳ ✳

COMFORTABLY NUMB

Unmistakable, right from the very first note, is the vastness this musical imagery connotes. The delay-sodden guitar slide up the neck easily evokes a sense of flight. Echoes place us somewhere in space. But instead of the outer hemispheres beyond the earth's bounds, "Comfortably Numb" takes us on a journey into the hemispheres of Pink's brain and the zenith of his now-altered consciousness.

Given the title's obvious nod to being stoned, we now see the effect of those narcotic references first presented in "Nobody Home;" it becomes a bit more obvious why the connective tissue of that particular song was written and added later in the recording process: to properly foreshadow this tragic moment in Pink's emotional downfall.

From the outright rock and roll circus hedonism of "Young Lust" to the dark reveal of what addictions and physical possessions are used to spackle the divots in Pink's soul in "Nobody Home" comes the arc of Corruption through Self-Medication that leads us here to Pink's nadir at the end of *The Wall*'s second act (which, also incidentally, is the end of Side 3 of the LP).

In cinematic three-act structure, the end of the second act is one of the most recognizable moments in the story arc. In short, it's the moment that despite all the things the protagonist has done on his journey, the worst has happened, leading to a point of immediate and dire crisis. In the movie *Jaws* it's the moment when the engine on Quint's boat dies, leaving the three men stranded in the middle of the ocean with no way to call for help and a very pissed off shark circling in the water below.

In "Comfortably Numb," Pink is trapped inside a whirlwind of emotional torment with no escape, facing the prospect of eternal living isolation similar to Joe Bonham in *Johnny Got His Gun*. With all control of his life now lost, he nearly overdoses on drugs.

"Comfortably Numb" was created from David Gilmour's music, Roger's lyric and Bob Ezrin's orchestral arrangement; the end result is something much greater than the sum of its parts. The song itself is possibly one of the greatest examples of pure rock and roll transcendence.

While there can be little questioning of the visual pictures of (altered) consciousness the music and arrangement paint in the listener's mind, it is the lyrics that form the deepest pool in which to let our minds wade.

Hello, is there anybody in there?
Just nod if you can hear me.
Is there anyone home?

At first it may appear that the lyrics Roger Waters sing here reflect the voice of a "doctor" and that David Gilmour's vocals reflect the voice of Pink.

There is no pain you are receding.
A distant ship, smoke on the horizon.
You are only coming through in waves.
Your lips move but I can't hear what you're saying.

However, given how this vocal dynamic has played out throughout the album so far, I'm now convinced this is a brilliant and devious twist that more accurately reflects the nature of duality in *The Wall*. The way Waters has created songs that seem to be one thing on the surface, but different upon scrutiny under the intellectual microscope, yield a possibility of separate interpretation.

I realize that in the movie adaptation of *The Wall*, this is where the band's manager, with a doctor in tow, breaks into Pink's room and the two are forced to resuscitate him. I don't deny that there obviously exists such a thread in the lyrics to "Comfortably Numb." However, it's also safe to say that the surreal nature of the movie lends itself to a more literal translation of those elements of fantasy within the narrative. You also have to take into account that movies and television don't have the luxury of allowing the onion to be gradually peeled back, layer by layer, and often have to shortcut the narrative to accomplish telling a story within the limited running time window of a couple hours, give or take.

Let's not forget that all the characters we have met that have been voiced by Waters and Gilmour represent Pink's own interpretations of these individuals and not the actual people themselves. It is only the groupie, the guy banging Pink's wife, and the telephone operator who were voiced by others — because they represent real people who enter the narrative and are not just figments of Pink's memory or imagination.

If this consistency in the presentation of these characters is to remain constant, one needs to consider the conclusion that Pink is only speaking to himself and *not* someone outside the wall. It is another simulacrum born of his psyche under the hallucinatory effects of narcotics.

Given how Waters' vocals take the first part of the song, this is also likely a conversation Pink is having with himself as his Super-Ego plays "doctor" to his wounded Id, with Gilmour singing the part of Pink's Ego, which contains regressed past — the inner child who doesn't understand what is happening to him.

Inside this cocoon of Pink's consciousness there is, in fact, a sort of metamorphosis underway. It would be folly to think that Pink could emerge from such an inner war without being changed. That's the foundation of the cinematic three-act story.

Hello, is there anybody in there?

Pink lives like a Russian nesting doll, inside one world that exists inside yet another. *Is there anybody out there...* As opposed to the mirror image question Pink asked just earlier at the end of "Bring the Boys Back Home," we have the "doctor" trying to diagnose whether his patient is all there and how far gone he may be. *Is there anybody home...* The "doctor's" inquiry expresses great doubt in his patient's sanity.

Come on, now, I hear you're feeling down.
Well I can ease your pain
And get you on your feet again.

This is obviously not a doctor faithful to his Hippocratic Oath (or any sort of ethical treatment of this particular patient). In fact, he only cares that his patient marches off to war, or in Pink's case, is be able to stay on his feet long enough to keep the well-oiled machine of rock stardom from grinding its gears. In this regard, the pressure Pink feels to keep his financial obligations, not only to himself but to the many who depend upon him for their daily bread, runs rather parallel with what Roger Waters must have felt while trying to finish *The Wall* under the crumbling of the band's interpersonal relationships and the rushed schedule placed upon him by their record company; if he failed, the financial future of Pink Floyd as a business entity would be in as much jeopardy as the *Titanic* on iceberg night.

Self-medicating to temporarily alleviate the feeling of being crushed by life's obligations isn't just a favored pastime of rich rock stars, and it's this ability to relate on some level to Pink's actions that wrings sympathy for his self-destructive impulses.

Can you show me where it hurts?

Given how internal this wound goes, it is fitting that metaphorically Pink has to become his own doctor to open himself up raw then become his own patient in order to expose his shattered psyche to himself. The self-realization of the illness's true depth is what causes Pink to purge himself of feeling anything, or to go numb.

There is no pain you are receding.
A distant ship, smoke on the horizon.
You are only coming through in waves.

When the Gilmour vocal comes in during the chorus, we've obviously switched to another perspective, this time that of the "patient." Given the internal difficulties going on with the band at the time, I don't know if it was a conscious decision on Roger Waters' part to consistently make David Gilmour the voice of the "Ego," but again we get the emergence of this part of Pink's psyche. At first, the Ego reinforces this sense of separation and isolation from the rest of Pink's consciousness. There is obviously no communication between the two. In the second half of the chorus, we delve into another of Freud's defense mechanisms: regression.

When I was a child I had a fever
My hands felt just like two balloons.

During "Nobody Home" we were introduced to the lament of "swollen hand blues," a complaint suffered by heroin addicts who shoot up into the veins of their hands to hide track marks.

Now I've got that feeling once again…

This regression into the persona of the "wounded child" takes us back to Pink's psychological ground zero. It is here, in childhood, where he suffers an illness so serious that it wasn't certain he would survive. The perspective of death's true finality bestowed upon him as a boy finally allows him to clearly understand the hole that will always be in his life because of his father's absence. The building of the wall is a result of trying to hide the hole from view, but as the hole widens, the wall must also grow. Nothing, not a smothering mother's love, nor fame, nor drugs, can fill the void. As the chasm deepens and the divide that separates his psyche from his being whole widens, the wall must go higher to hide it.

So now, behind the wall, Pink falls into the void.

I have become comfortably numb.

This first guitar solo launches on a wailing note. Though it is a precursor for the epic solo Gilmour unleashes later after the second chorus, there is an uplifting sense that the guitar is singing a song for itself. There is not so much virtuosity here as there is feeling. The extended sustained notes that Gilmour lands on at the top of every other bar are derived from the 3rd of the root chord, giving us tension and the 5th, which connotes that strong heroic-sounding resolution. Behind this, audible in the mix, are Ezrin's cellos playing beautiful descending phrases that give the proceedings a very pastoral and calm exterior.

Okay, just a little pinprick.

There'll be no more…aaaaaaaaah!

But you may feel a little sick.

As heroin enters the bloodstream, the body's receptors are flooded by opioids. The resulting feeling includes nausea, vomiting, dizziness. The abstract clues that point toward heroin demonstrate how Pink is not having these conversations with someone outside the wall, such as the doctor seen in the movie version, but instead with *himself*; he is self-medicating and still very alone.

Listen also to the way the "aaaaaaaaah!" is sung in the frenetic Pink voice. This is the voice of the present Pink. This is the sound of his reaction to the needle going into his vein.

Then the "prescribed" shot starts working. Pink has rendered himself functional enough to venture forth and fulfill his professional obligations once more, assuming the mask of rock star Pink.

As we enter the second chorus, there is another a separation and lack of communication, but here it takes quite an interesting turn.

Listen closely in the recording to the orchestra during this lyric in the chorus.

Your lips move but I can't hear what you're saying.

In the mix, there is a French horn playing a three note phrase that spans from the root note to the 5th and then up a perfect 4th to the octave where it began. This is a mirror image of Strauss' epic *Also Sprach Zarathustra*. It is this line in the orchestral arrangement that lends a suggestion of transcendence and the continuation of Pink's metamorphosis.

When I was a child I caught a fleeting glimpse
Out of the corner of my eye.
I turned to look but it was gone
I cannot put my finger on it now

Did he see his own place in the world? Being walked upon by those authority figures who would only tear his self-esteem to pieces because they were overcompensating for something? Did he see the possibility of his own death? Perhaps it was the grim reaper lurking just out of the corner of his eye?

Or could it have been the ghost of his dead father?

Since it's a vision that can't be described, did Waters intentionally give a nod back to the song "Mother" (also the sixth song on its half of *The Wall* and the only other song in the entire album that has a silent gap — both before and — after rather than being audibly connected to the next song)? Is this just another hypothetical question that can never truly be answered?

Given the regression that occurs again upon the mention of that fleeting glimpse from childhood, this transcendence seems to suggest a rebirth of consciousness, possibly similar to the one experienced at the end of the movie *2001: A Space Odyssey* where the Strauss piece played such an overwhelming role. The bigger question then becomes this: could what Pink describes seeing as a boy have instead been God?

In the same way that drug users have been known to associate their spiritual journeys of altered consciousness with the search to "see God," does Pink turn to heroin in order to revisit this moment of unanswered questions from the psychological ground zero of his childhood? The moment eludes his grasp like quicksilver running through his fingers, like the fading echo of a tolling bell. To understand what that seminal memory actually meant could lead to the resolution of his lifelong issues. Though he tries to find it again, it is gone... forever.

Those tolling bells metaphorically come alive around 4:25, right before the second guitar solo. The bass plays two bars, pounding that D note with steady quarter note rhythm, subconsciously calling our attention to the coming of a message of great importance.

One that arrives in the form of a guitar solo that blisters with the passion of a desperate voice fighting to be heard.

Voted by the readers of "Guitar Player Magazine" to be the fourth greatest guitar solo of all time (Number one was, predictably, Jimmy Pages' immaculately-conceived guitar slinging in "Stairway to Heaven"), it's safe to say this is the most signature moment from all of David Gilmour's six-string work. There's every reason to believe that the unstable relationship Gilmour had with Waters during this period in the band's history played an emotional role here as well. With Waters taking control of Pink Floyd and essentially turning it into *his* band to record *his* album, there is an undeniable sense of urgency in what Gilmour played.

Brilliantly edited together from several takes Gilmour had recorded, the second solo in "Comfortably Numb" is composed of a number of scorching licks that, unlike the song's first solo, don't dynamically build up to a crescendo but instead come out swinging right from the gate. Now if the grand build in the solo after the first chorus and all of the heroic-sounding root-to-perfect 5th jumps made the sound "angelic," then this heavily blues-driven solo is the "brimstone and fire" of that devil sitting on Pink's other shoulder.

In Freudian terms, it even goes deeper. That angelic solo represents Pink's Super-Ego, the part of his psyche that includes his spiritual goals, the psychic energy commonly called the "conscience," and his ego ideals — the inner self-image one wants to become. That second, darker solo then that represents Pink's Id. Within this unconscious stew of primal instincts and desires resides, of course, the libido and the inaccessible part of the human personality — that boiling cauldron of chaos, full of seething expectations and quite unresponsive to the demands and earthly bounds of reality.

Represented in this nearly two-minute long fire-breathing feast of screaming transcendental emotion is the culmination of Pink's metamorphosis.

From this battle between the angel on one shoulder and the devil on the other, comes the newly reborn Pink. As he emerges fully-formed from his womb-like isolation, it will become clear that it is the devil that has won and that Pink's Id has gained control.

✹✹✹✹

THE SHOW MUST GO ON

Musically, we are whisked back in time via a tune that sounds artfully inspired by the 50's, complete with a falsetto wail that treads on the mental real estate owned by "The Lion Sleeps Tonight" and other familiar do-wop classics. It is fitting that here, at the point of rebirth and the consequences it will bring, we metaphorically revisit the influence of Pink's parents and the era of Pink's youth. Welcome to the beginning of Act Three in the story arc to *The Wall.*

Ooooh, Ma, Oooh Pa

Must the show go on?

Originally published in 1961, Michael Foucault's seminal tome *Madness and Civilization: A History of Insanity in the Age of Reason* defines madness as an object of perception within a social space. French philosopher Foucault observed that during the Renaissance the mad were protected by their families and viewed as possessing a certain wisdom — the essence between what men are and what they pretend to be. During the Classical Age, the insane were institutionalized and finally, here in the Modern Age, insanity is treated through medication that allows those suffering to exist within the boundaries of society without disrupting the flow.

The layered meanings of the message are clear. Pink has self-medicated with heroin in order to put on the mask and function in the professional capacity expected of his famous rock star persona. But with the inevitable visit from his own Dickensian Ghost of Christmas Yet-To-Come, the show in question is a tormented play presented to him, on this dark night of the soul, that he can't bear to watch any longer. Yet, he must: such is the nature of life and as such, the "show" is a direct metaphor for his life. It must go on.

Oooh Pa... Take me home.

In "the show," his life flashes before his eyes: first as a baby, then quickly as a boy. It was Carl Jung, the father of analytic psychiatry, who postulated that a patient's regressive tendency is not just a relapse into infantilism, but an attempt to get at something necessary such as the universal feeling of childhood curiosity, security, and reciprocated love and trust.

Do not mistake this as Pink longing for the innocence of youth and the protection afforded him at mother's bosom.

Oooh Ma... Let me go.

Pink saying "take me home" to his long-in-the-grave father and "let me go" to his oft-clinging mother to, might lead one to think he's asking the ghosts of his parents to give him permission to die. Pink contemplating suicide — while probable in his emotionally-eviscerated state — is something Waters has carefully steered clear of in the narrative so far. Sure, just saying "Goodbye Cruel World" is, to some extent, cliché pop-culture shorthand for "I'm going to kill myself." However, I don't think there's ever any of that intention to highlight suicide as an option for Pink. His "death" is strictly metaphorical.

Instead, what dies is his sense of self; it is the rest of his soul that dangles on a gossamer thread between a metaphorical heaven and hell. Like Ebenezer Scrooge before him, visiting his own long-gone past while disembodied from his consciousness, Pink cries out to the ghosts of his parents. He asks his father to take him home. He pleads with the smothering mother to let him go. Both are things he never did in his past life.

Listen closely underneath the echoing background vocals and you'll hear a synth (layered with guitar) playing an alternating two-note riff, C to G# — a dissonant interval that is reminiscent of the siren on a European-style ambulance possibly like the one Waters' father drove during The Blitz. This then begs the question of whether the tom tom hits are an audio production metaphor meant to represent explosions of anti-aircraft fire. In either case, the sound exists to highlight a warning. At this point, Pink's existence is renewed, but he is fundamentally changed. This subliminal siren underpins a sense of caution and that even in the metaphorical ambulance, this patient is still sick.

There must be some mistake
I didn't mean to let them take away my soul.
Am I too old, is it too late?

During this bridge, the song switches meter from its initial 4/4 meter to 3/4. signifying a change in perspective. Here, having seen the "show" playing in his head (like Scrooge), Pink becomes introspective and finally has an epiphany about what has happened to him. These things we, the listeners, have been privy to, are finally understood by Pink in his own "a-ha" moment. The lyrics about the theft of his soul apply evenly across many aspects of his life: school, the record companies and even, to some extent, the audience.

All the while, Pink's palpitating heartbeat, as portrayed by the bass guitar's erratic rhythm, further ads to the emotional tension of the moment.

There's another interesting twisted-mirror dynamic going on here as well. In the anti-war novel *Johnny Got His Gun*, one of the most memorable and emotionally heavy ideas that author Dalton Trumbo sets forth is that the soldier, when laying injured and dying, thinks not of the noble and heroic sacrifice made in war, but instead cries for his mother and begs to be saved. By that criteria, while the first part "The Show Must Go On" — where Pink asks to be "taken home" and "let go" — connotes a certain embrace of death, there is also this complete 180 degree twist during the bridge where he's lyrically pleading for another chance. In some regard, this could even the voice of Pink's father expressing his last regrets as he lays dying on a battlefield far away from his family, lamenting that he's starting to lose feeling in his body and understanding that the show, whether it's the war itself, or life (as its own "show") continues on without him.

Ooooh, Ma, Ooooh Pa,
Where has the feeling gone?

The "feeling" is gone because, as we left him in the last song, he's numb - though possibly not comfortably anymore. Because there are so many instances in *The Wall* where lyrics in one song help expand and reveal meaning of those in another song, we finally are allowed the obvious connection between being numb and having no feeling.

Remember, the reason for Pink to numb himself is as an attempt to end his own suffering. However, the side effects are that he has lost *all* feeling. Without feeling, particularly suffering, there can be no compassion.

Without feeling, there can be no artistry, either.

Will I remember the song?

Being numb, he's in a bit of a crisis. His rock star confidence has vanished. He has a great hesitation about stepping out onto that stage. Yet again, this hesitation also applies to allowing the "show" that has become his life (both inside and outside of his mind) to continue.

The show must go on…

This, the oldest and possibly best known of theatrical sayings, is how Waters chooses to button the song. Kinetically, it propels us forward in the narrative by implying that nobody here is quitting. Pink's tentative first steps in his rebirth will be taken. But because of the length of *The Wall* and the overall complexity of its abstract narrative, Rogers is also seemingly speaking to that part of the audience that may be confused, as well as to those who feel that the dizzying heights of "Comfortably Numb" surely marked the climax of the album. Not so. Instead, he's reassuring those who care that in order to find out what happens next to Pink, all we have to do is sit in the audience and listen.

Oddly enough, the original production concept was for the Beach Boys to sing the harmonies. Lending their wholesome tone to a song that finds Pink stuck in the no-man's land between salvation and damnation (a dark concept to say the least!) would have subliminally given it a special twisted mirror irony similar to the military band-style arrangement for an anti-war song in "Bring the Boys Back Home."

However, it was not to be. The recording session was scheduled for October 2, 1979; that morning, after finally recognizing the themes of *The Wall*, Mike Love called to cancel. Given the Beach Boys' similar experiences dealing with a lead songwriter gone crazy from neurosis, drugs and isolation, one would think Love would be sympathetic. However, all Syd Barrett/

Brian Wilson comparisons aside, Love — not known to be the most congenial or warmhearted of fellows — declined the invite at the last moment. Though the session had to be rescheduled for a week later, Waters was able to wrangle Beach Boy Bruce Johnston, along with backup singers John Joyce, Joe Chemay, Stan Farber, session singer Jim Haas, and the one and only Toni Tenille (of Cap'n and Tenille fame). The rich and dynamic harmonies of their voices carry us through a song that signifies a switch in the narrative's motif from transcendence to destiny — one whose path remains unalterable like a bullet fired from a gun or a bomb dropped from the sky.

※ ※ ※ ※ ※

IN THE FLESH

The drumsticks click together, marking the countdown to an explosion on a darkened stage once again. We are back at the rock show, the spectacle. Here again is Pink on stage, in the flesh for all to see. It is another night and another stop on the tour; the music hasn't really changed nor has our space cadet glow. Instead it is Pink who is now different. As side one's "In the Flesh?" introduced us to Pink's real life, we now have a nearly identical thundering march shine the spotlight on the persona that has emerged from the metamorphosis.

"In The Flesh?" and "In the Flesh" are nearly identical and feature the exact same guitar riff and arrangement, leaving one to wonder if the two were part of the same take. Lay the audio waveforms on top of each other and they match up perfectly until the fifth bar after the second "march," when the second one slows slightly. Whereas "In the Flesh?" has vocals that come in after the intro, side two's version has a sixteen bar interlude of harmonized voices. Once again, we are visited by very pleasant sounding Beach Boys-inspired voices and clean 50's-style musical arrangement. These elements, borrowed from a much simpler era, evoke a sense of being uncorrupted. It becomes very subversive though, because while you have this pleasant, somewhat happy sounding major key music, it contains this awful, dark message. In many ways, it mirrors how Waters feels Vera Lynn and her happy-sounding music were used to drive propaganda under a subliminal veneer of whitewash.

Like many songs from *The Wall*, "In The Flesh" is part of a mirrored pair comprised of a light half and a dark half. Needless to say... this is the dark half.

Though the first four lines of lyrics are exactly same as the first time we've heard them, what comes next gives us our first clue how far the ship has gone off course into open seas.

I've got some bad news for you, sunshine,
Pink isn't well, he stayed back at the hotel

Sunshine is, of course, the ultimate form of light. As a metaphor, light is commonly representative of the truth. Let us now again remember that this isn't an actual rock concert, but the further extension of "the show" playing in Pink's mind during this dark night of his soul. The bad news isn't so much that "sunshine" (meaning happiness) is left standing outside the velvet rope of Pink's psyche as it is Pink's Id taunting his Ego.

He's letting us know that Pink's separation from reality is now complete. He's gone off the deep end and Pink is another person. The Id is in charge.

We're gonna find out where you fans really stand.

In the same way that Pink took accounting of the mere physical objects that defined his life in "Nobody Home," here, in this packed house, he will assess his audience. At the end of the second act, during "Comfortably Numb," Pink had the drug-fueled realization that he could not "see" what lay just hidden from his vision because he was not worthy. For him to understand what exists for him beyond this world required an ascendancy to a higher conscience, free of the earthly bounds of the human world.

Earthly bounds like feelings — the things that make Pink vulnerable and weak.

From the pupa and larval stage comes the birth of a butterfly, born of complete insanity, to be known as "Dictator Pink." Because he has ascended, he is the only one capable of judging who is worthy.

Are there any queers in the theater tonight?
Get them up against the wall.

It is the Id-driven persona of Dictator Pink that has finally wrested control. Unlike Powerless Pink who uses his fame to try and fill an un-fillable void in his soul, Dictator Pink will use his cult of personality to drive his followers to become an unblinking army of drones.

That one looks Jewish!
And that one's a coon!
Who let all of this riff-raff into the room?

Though quite inflammatory in nature, the next two lines asking about the other riff-raff who are smoking a joint (or, absurdly, covered in spots) helps define all of the stuff about "Coons" and "Jews" as obvious sarcasm and make it perfectly clear these are the rantings of a madman. Dictator Pink is trying to foment his own revolution. This one is not based upon the values of the individual; now he is commanding his followers to blindly pledge allegiance to a world where the uniformed prohibition of free thought becomes institutionalized and people are stigmatized by race, creed, color, individual ability, accomplishment or otherwise standing out from the herd.

The irony, of course, is that this is exactly the type of authoritarian mentality that he rebelled against in the hallowed halls of his education — the same mindset decried over an educational system that tried to break his spirited individuality. The threat of a dystopian future that he once feared and rebelled against has become something he has embraced.

Now the bullied has become the bully.

Growing up, Pink was made to feel neutered by his overbearing, smothering (though well-intentioned) mother, and then later emasculated by his cruel teachers. That those teachers were themselves bullied by their own overlords (fat and psychopathic wives) speaks to the metaphor about the tendency of the powerless wanting to turn into the bully (the powerful) because of the human psyche's difficulty in breaking away from the evil that others have done; thus, we are condemned to futures of blindly reliving and repeating those childhood experiences. The victim becomes the perpetrator when the emotionally-scarring ordeals of one's past determine that they are unable to act with compassion to others.

Obviously, Waters is drawing a parallel between isolation, self-loathing, and the genesis of fascist thinking. The delusions we are certain are afflicting Pink mirror the mindset of a madman like Hitler or Mussolini. One little known historical fact is that Hitler himself was bullied intensely by a strictly disciplinarian father who bore a bad temper. The constant beatings Hitler received as a boy would later be passed along after his father's death when teenaged Adolph began to use his fists on his younger sister, Paula.

Because *The Wall* is an album that is obsessed with both cause and effect, once you hear "In the Flesh" and understand the context, the crowd noise in the song begins to sound less like a rock show and more like a Nuremburg rally. Waters has consistently shown propaganda's ill effects, be it those little white lies from mother, the educational system's indoctrination to becoming a good employee or Vera Lynn's siren songs pedaling the faux nobility of going off to war and dying. In each of these examples, the lie becomes a virus that sprouts and blooms within the hearts and minds of those who fall under its spell.

Psychologically speaking, those who participate in a "mob" mentality often experience *deindividuation*, otherwise known as a complete loss of self-awareness in groups. Someone who deindividuates is prone to loss of inhibition and, even more sinister, a loss of their sense of individual identity.

More than just megalomaniacal dictators get drawn into this parallel. To some extent, though only lightly implied, there's sense here that through Pink's epiphany of what he saw as a child out of the corner of his eye during "Comfortably Numb," he has become, in some ways, Divine. The threat of authoritarian rule under a cult of personality that deindividuates its followers is not exclusive to the secular world.

We know what happened in Nazi Germany. We can only imagine what will happen in the mock fascist Reich of Dictator Pink's mind.

If I had my way, I'd have all of you shot!

In 1939, French existentialist philosopher and novelist John Paul Sarte published a book of short stories called: you guessed it, *The Wall.*

Inside this book, the eponymously-titled first story is about a man named Pablo who finally finds meaning in his life in the hours before he is about to be executed by the firing squad of an authoritarian regime. Sartre wrote "The Wall" using a first-person, stream-of-consciousness point-of-view. There are other characters in the story but their dialogue is filtered through Pablo's mind as recollection. Isolated inside a jail cell, there is a sense of terror that slowly unfolds inside of Pablo's psyche.

Sound familiar?

To Sartre, the nature of humankind is defined by the consequences of responsibility, including the anguish over making decisions, the sense of abandonment in trying to make it alone, and the despair felt when it all goes wrong. Life demands commitment to a path whose significance will constantly remain open to doubt.

When you apply this general philosophy to the difficulties and extreme pressure Waters experienced in trying to create this album, there is definitely something *very* familiar about it.

Sartre's "The Wall" defines the nature of self-betrayal as our desire to often mold ourselves into becoming what others want us to be rather than who we truly are. It was only the immanence of his impending death that allowed the true nature of human life to be revealed to Pablo. Despite all of life's anguish over responsibility, self-deception, and despair, in the end who we truly are is all that counts.

However, Dictator Pink is far from the clarity he will need to rescue him from this path he has taken. The pampered rock star surrounded by sycophants has assumed a "chosen one" role and made commands of those who follow.

And now the Id is dangerously unleashed.

* * * * *

RUN LIKE HELL

Bouncing from fingers of David Gilmour's heavily delayed guitar, they come: ricochets!

Welcome to your dystopian future!

This time it's not Nuremberg. Instead, a rock crowd chants, "Pink! Floyd! Pink! Floyd!" From this comes the familiar Morse code of that single-picked and heavily echoed D note, followed soon after by Gilmour's jangly and flanged guitar chords ringing out like the tolling of bells.

Ringing and calling.

These metaphorical bells have appeared in previous songs from the narrative that announced the three most important stages of Pink's isolation. "Another Brick In The Wall (Part 3)" marked the moment Pink completed his wall. "Goodbye Cruel World" announced his choice to stay behind that wall and "Comfortably Numb" signaled his abandonment of reality.

The Morse code-like picked guitar, like the kind heard in "Another Brick In The Wall (Part 1)," "The Happiest Days Of Our Lives," and "Another Brick In The Wall (Part 3)" has generally shown up at moments where past transgressions were being called out and assigned blame. And by "past," we're talking about recollections of instances from Pink's youth.

So it would stand to reason that such a strong and present combination of these two metaphorical elements not only underscores the importance of the upcoming message, but also to signal that "Run Like Hell" will somehow thematically tie in with actions from the past, as well as warn about yet another stage of isolation upcoming.

What he's talking about here is *the crumbling of civilization as we know it...* and the warning signs that very well may precede it.

Run. Run. Run. Run. Run Run. Run. Run....

On the surface, and within the scope of the narrative of *The Wall* to this point, "Run Like Hell" seems like the all-points-bulletin being issued by demagogue Dictator Pink to his enemies; however, it goes much further than that. Yes, I realize that the movie version of *The Wall* features skinheads (a.k.a "fascism's street team") running wild and carrying out Pink's desired New World Order. But it would be a mistake to think Alan Parker's vision is a complete translation of the song as originally intended, especially given how symbolically rich the entire album is from beginning to end.

If it were just Pink banging his shoe on the podium, the song would be about how the symptoms of delusion can spread like a virus from one person to many. While that may be true, "Run Like Hell" follows the motif in *The Wall* of not just being about cause, but also of *effect*. Remember, we are still actually in Pink's head; this is his visit from his own Ghost of Christmas Future.

You better make your face up in your favorite disguise.
With your button down lips and your roller blind eyes.

Chasing the vocal, just one beat behind is an echo of itself. This delayed doppelganger gives us the musical equivalent of a "Dutch angle" in cinema where the shot is framed slightly skewed to imply that the events being witnessed are off-kilter.

The use of the pronoun "you" is as an intentionally subliminal prompt for your ears to pick up. In the same regard that "Hey You" not only reflects a poetic recap of the narrative, but also stands as a direct message to the audience to be aware of signs of mental issues caused by self-isolation, "Run Like Hell" also breaks the fourth wall so that Waters may speak to you face-to-face. He's trying to be the anti-Vera Lynn. Waters is using his fame to directly deliver this warning about conflict as opposed to being yet another opiate that renders the masses comfortably numb to the threat of conflict.

One may choose to believe that an Orwellian-style dystopian future under a totalitarian regime is fantasy or not; here, Waters has drawn a line in the narrative that connects such a divergent dot with the outlying concepts of fascism run amok. Let us not forget that the path towards a Huxley-esque Brave New World and banning/burning of books a' la *Fahrenheit 451,* along with the persecution of those who stood to threaten the Reich, were among Hitler's ultimate goals.

If left to fester, how different would a fascist future be?

Waters is asking you to imagine it.

Imagine hiding who you truly are so as to not draw unwanted attention to anything that may be construed as different. Imagine keeping your mouth shut and eyes averted.

Imagine watching anxiously in silence as civilization crumbles.

With your nerves in tatters as the cockle shell shatters.
And the hammers batter down your door.

Fascinating how this one lyric particularly suggests a thematic relationship with another famous story of isolation, William Golding's epic *Lord of the Flies*, a novel about a group of British schoolboys who are evacuated during wartime only to have their plane shot down, leaving them stranded on a deserted island.

A fable of order vs. chaos, reason vs. desire and, ultimately, good vs. evil, *Lord of the Flies* is about the conflict within all humans between the instinct to live by the rules and the impulse to break them in order to satisfy one's immediate desire for control. In the story, there is a white conch shell (a type of cockle shell) that is *extremely* symbolic of the castaways ability to maintain a civilized state of existence.

Two of the boys, Piggy and Ralph, discover the white conch shell on the beach. "Careful! You'll break it!" cries Piggy as Ralph goes to pick it up. The shell exists as a metaphor for civilization, and Piggy shows prophetic concern over its fragility and how one wrong move could cause it to shatter. A later conversation about how much such a tropical treasure would cost back home is symbolic of the price people are willing to pay for civilization.

The conch shell is used as a horn to be blown, a signal to summon the other boys, and as such symbolizes the birth of civilization. It is the shell that governs their meetings; he who holds the conch shell holds the right to speak. But as their island civilization erodes in a struggle for power, the act of holding the conch shell loses its influence. Once it is stripped as a totem of power, it stands symbolic of civilization's decay. Finally, amidst complete chaos, the conch shell is shattered and along with it, all remaining civilization.

Interesting though is the dynamic of the human psyche. The boys become Id-driven by their basic needs and desires. They brutally kill a pig based on the natural instinct of hunger. They go to the bathroom wherever they choose. The Super Ego compels them to create a government. Soon, the Ego makes its play when the group splits in two and certain members choose to join the new group only to not anger the leader. These are the things that make *Lord of the Flies* such a fascinating parable about the inner struggles of the unchecked human psyche. In the end, the boys' loss of innocence is not the result of them being changed by something that was done *to* them; rather, it is the natural result of their continuing acceptance of the innate darkness and savagery that had always existed deep inside them.

From that isolation came monsters.

What do you do when monsters appear?

You better run.

Into the mix, enter bongos and a conga, the Latin percussion signifying that it's a jungle out there.

The mention of "dirty feelings" brings us back to those kinds of girls that Mother would never let get through and the ones that young Pink was looking for in the rock and roll circus of debauchery. Because Waters wants to leave no threat to personal freedom untouched by the gift of his spotlight, the type persecution that comes under attack here is that done on moral grounds.

Cause if they catch you in the back seat trying to pick her locks,

They're gonna send you back to mother in a cardboard box.

In reference to sexual acts that may be construed as immoral, this feels less grounded in political and ideological issues than it does in religious control. Obviously a touchy issue, Waters makes just enough of this imagery to subversively get his point across: the potential threat to personal freedoms may not come from not just the state but, to some extent, from the church as well.

Take a look at the very last words of each line in the first verse.

Disguise.
Eyes.
Heart.
Past.
Tatters.
Shatters.
Door.

In this order, they are subliminally evocative of the narrative that takes place during the first half of *The Wall*.

Now look at the very last words of each line in the second verse.

Night.
Inside.
Tonight.
Sight.
Locks.
Box.

These definitely evoke a sense of the narrative of the second half after Pink has shut himself away behind this wall of his creation.

Cause and effect.

You better run.

Notice how the word "run" echoes, ping-ponging left to right, emphasizing this command as the synthesizer solo comes to life with a pitch and distinct vibrato eerily reminiscent of a gritty theremin. An electronic musical instrument developed in 1919, the theremin actually has no keys or strings. Instead, it reads the position of the player's hands in between two antennae and converts the interference of the electronic field into pitch and amplitude, creating musical notes.

Famously used in the music for the doomsday movie *The Day the Earth Stood Still,* the theremin is the epitome of classic science-fiction. The theremin is often used to evoke tension, danger and mystery within the realm of a perceived future. That also holds true here in "Run Like Hell;" this theremin-tone is meant to be as ominous as any end of the world scenario.

Hurried footfalls on the run bridge the end of the solo, soon followed by a maniacal laugh and the sound of madness in the night. These echoing steps flee from the madmen who intend harm. Soon we hear the screeching of tires, more laughter. The pursuit is on. At approximately 4:00, the running stops and there is a quick, sharp inhale and exhale. Out of breath.

Roger Waters' screeching hawk shriek swoops in; it is no mild coincidence that a familiar, aggressive bird-of-prey cry preceded the dystopian breeding ground of "Another Brick In The Wall (Part 3)" or the similarity of the two songs' blind marching tempo and beat.

Cause and effect. Greed for power over others corrupts.

Like the very cyclical nature of *The Wall*, we come back to where we started; a crowd rallying around a cult of personality and the musical Morse code, and the tolling of bells.

Ringing and calling.

While Pink/Roger could not get his wife to answer his calls because he did not know how to communicate with her, Waters is hoping he doesn't make the same mistake with us, the audience, in letting us know this is a warning that demands to be heard.

*****

WAITING FOR THE WORMS

To a hammer, everything looks like a nail.

So goes an old saying that explains the nature of the authoritarian mindset. In a world where a jackboot held down across one's throat constitutes political discourse, he who has the power makes the rules. After over 6,000 or so years of history, one thing is quite clear: men desire power so they can control, conquest and manipulate.

Those who dare stand in the way get beaten down.

Like a nail that needs driving.

Eins, zwei, drei, alle!

No longer cheering the name of their favorite band, the crowd's unison chant is now "Hammer! Hammer!" Once again, it evokes that Nuremberg rally feeling. The count off in German foreshadows another goose-step march from our resident proto-fascist, Dictator Pink. It is the Beach Boys-style Greek chorus that delivers the bad news. The message is simple: Pink has now mentally gone past the point of no return.

You cannot reach me now.

No matter how you try.

Goodbye cruel world. It's over.

Walk on by...

As the rhythmic beat of the bass drum evokes a heavy clock, marking time, it is hard to escape that the next two lines, traded off between Gilmour and Waters, evoke a direct comparison to the finality of Hitler's downward spiral.

(Gilmour) *Sitting in a bunker here behind my wall.*

(Waters) *Waiting for the worms to come...*

With his plans to reshape the world in his image foiled and his army on its heels, it was a similar subterranean lair known as the Führerbunker near Berlin's Reich Chancellery where Hitler spent his final weeks, hiding from the quickly advancing Allied forces. With surrender inevitable, the Fürher would put a pistol to his head and blow his brains out.

Gilmour and Waters again trade lines in the next couplet.

(Gilmour) *In perfect isolation behind my wall.*

(Waters) *Waiting for the worms to come...*

Previously, in *The Wall,* when the vocalist changed, it signified a shift in perspective. During "Comfortably Numb", Gilmour sang the lyrics that represented the Ego portion of Pink's psyche; the same holds true here. Pink's Ego is highlighted in the two lines Gilmour sings as it continues to put up and justify a defense mechanism. The Ego is content to be safe, even at such a high cost. To some extent, the use of the word "perfect" to describe the isolation even represents a shifting to the Super -Ego, the part of the psyche that aims for perfection. It's a subtle acceptance that signifies further erosion of Pink's emotional.

But where there is Gilmour's Ego (and Super-Ego), there must be balance. Who better to provide the devil to Pink's shoulder angel than Roger Waters as the Id?

Worms feast on decomposing matter. Worms eat dead bodies. From the Id comes the pervasive layers of darkness that make "Waiting for the Worms" a nadir for Pink. At first, he is "waiting for the worms to come," seemingly for the end of his life to take him into its sweet and permanent embrace. However, he is not a man waiting to die; he is a man who has lost his humanity. As the lyric soon changes to "waiting to *follow* the worms," it becomes clear these slimy dirt dwellers form some sort of advancing army; one that will "cut out the deadwood," "clean up the city," and "weed out the weaklings."

Invoking these worms is not just to create a symbol of death, but of *becoming* Death itself — the Grim Reaper.

The plague of intolerance that begat Nazism and the subsequent persecution and murder of millions becomes the thematic backdrop for what Waters has to say about the dangers of isolationism and totalitarianism. The black shirt, smashed windows, and kicked in doors are eerily reminiscent of Mussolini's fascist paramilitary supporters and *Kristallnacht*, a pogrom against Jews throughout Germany (coordinated by Hitler's Brownshirts). Waiting for "the final solution," "to turn on the showers," and "fire the ovens," are undeniable references to the Holocaust, as is the satirically derogatory list of undesirables that follows.

Though the sensible person would recoil at these horrible, genocidal ravings and believe it could never happen where they lived, Waters deftly uses Gilmour's shoulder angel to ask:

Would you like to see Britannia rule again, my friend?

The faded empire returned to its former glory as rulers of the civilized world.

All you have to do is follow the worms… answers the Id. To rule over all, you must be a hammer, ready to crush anything that gets in your way.

But it goes much deeper. The two-bar *Twilight Zone*-esque distorted guitar riff appears here briefly to foreshadow a mind-blowing twist.

Would you like to send our coloured cousins home again, my friend?

The use of Gilmour's shoulder angel to ask such a surprisingly racist thing, as well as the consistent attempt to associate this question as coming from a "friend," is an extremely clever method of illuminating how the seeds of such isolationist thinking can originate even from sources close and familiar. In particular, it brings to mind an extreme nationalist political party started in Great Britain back in 1932 called The British Union of Fascists. After a visit to Italy and spending time with Benito Mussolini, British Labor Party minister Sir Oswald Mosley created the BUF, borrowing heavily from the Blackshirts. Basic principles of BUF beliefs revolved around the concept of isolating Britain from the rest of the world in terms of culture and commerce.

One shudders at the thought of how different history could have been had those worms been followed.

From here, the Twilight Zone-esque distorted guitar riff returns. By echoing the notes from the verse of "Another Brick In The Wall (Part 2)" — *We don't need no education. We don't need no thought control...* — Waters evokes the negative facets of Pink's youth and the oppressiveness of authoritarian conformity. Not only does he once again subtly point a finger at an educational system with an assembly line mentality, but also uses it to make a subliminal commentary that the megaphone fascists and Nuremberg mob mentality becomes ingrained into a society at an early age in an attempt to normalize it.

Here the mob chants, "Hammer! Hammer!" and searches for a nail.

As the crowd gets louder and louder, reaching a cacophonous fever pitch, the music finally gets drowned out.

So we return to that moment on the Montreal stage that birthed *The Wall* in Roger Waters' mind. Overpowered by a crowd that only cared to make noise, Waters' music became lost in the mob, causing him to spit in the face of an unruly concert goer in a moment of temporary megalomania.

As this typhoon swirl of insanity devolves into complete madness and chaos and reaches its frenzied climax, there is light — a moment of clarity. From the darkness of Pink's self-imposed imprisonment, his conscience reawakens as his mouth releases a halting cry!

Stop!

✳ ✳ ✳ ✳ ✳

STOP

I wanna go home.
Take off this uniform and leave the show.

Just piano and voice, stripped away of any ornamentation or affectations, Pink is laid bare and exposed to us and the world. As opposed to the depth-laden openness of the final mixes of "Hey You," "Comfortably Numb," and "Run Like Hell," the quick tail off of the reverb from the vocal along with the sharpened highs of the piano tone in "Stop" make it seem like we have now found ourselves locked inside a dank, stone cube-like room — wholly appropriate, given Pink's location.

But I'm waiting in this cell because I have to know,
Have I been guilty all this time?

We finally reach Pink's sudden and deep understanding of a truth that has so far been beyond his grasp. At last, his vision has become unclouded by an epiphany and a revelation. Referred to by people suffering from addictions as a "moment of clarity," it is the instant that allows them to see through the fog of their substance problem and realize they need to stop and get help.

Shockingly, this is the first time Pink has *directly* let out a cry for help. During "One of My Turns," his much-stunted attempt to connect with the groupie was a very *indirect* cry for help that nearly ended up being as much of a disaster as the moment the monster in "Frankenstein" tried to befriend the little girl, only inadvertently drown her.

Finally Pink, in his own voice, admits he's ready to go home; in essence, calling out for mommy and saying he's ready to leave this delusion behind. Again we get the theatrical reference to life as a "show." The multi-layering of this imagery doesn't just pertain to the costume of a dictator or a stage that Pink (or Roger) inhabits as a celebrity rock star and the destructive influences that follow in its shadows; this "play" being put on in his mind requires that he revisit his deepest and most hurtful neuroses. The repetition of the same four bar piano figure turns it into sort of a mantra. This is a moment of transcendence back to a state of physical being.

Within every good story is the search for some sort of universal truth. The "cell" in question is a clear metaphor for the self-imposed imprisonment behind the wall of isolation built by Pink's own psyche. The way the lyric "have to know" is echoed and repeated in the mix indicates this search for truth. Subsequently, the echoing repeats of "time" emphasize that the moment for truth is now.

By questioning his possible guilt for the crimes that have put him where he is, he acknowledges that from the fog comes the emergence of his conscience.

More importantly, it symbolizes a victory of the Super-Ego, the part of the psyche that maintains our sense of morality, of what is right and what is wrong.

The Super-Ego is formed by identifying with the internalization of the father figure. This is the signal that Pink is no longer dominated by the defense mechanisms of the helpless child of his Ego. Having seen the ravages created by his Mr. Hyde-like Id, Pink steps out from behind the shadow of his father's ghost. This is monumental. It is the moment he becomes a man.

Riding in like the emotional cavalry to save him from his own doom, Pink's conscience emerges with a newfound sense of accountability. It is said the first step to recovery is admitting there is a problem. Whereas before there was the finger-point of blame, finally comes this glimmer of culpability in his own downfall.

It took the recognition of his isolation, first behind a wall and later inside a bunker, as a prison offering only an eventual lonely death while "waiting for the worms." In the same way that Sartre's existentialist protagonist in his short story "The Wall" emerges from the angst and despair of his imprisonment and impending execution knowing he will soon die, Pink finds authenticity; he regains his ability to reconcile with his flawed self. He chooses to no longer be one who is only defined by his own past.

The final message here is clear: realize you are an individual, an independent and conscious being, rather than a stereotype or product of a preconceived notion. Do not let your Ego and Id subsume your Super-Ego. Let your conscience be your guide.

*****

THE TRIAL

At first blush it would seem that *The Wall* is a fable about the decay of individuality through isolation and the hopeful rise of the individual as a result of the common bond of humanity.

But that would be selling it short.

At its core, it's about deindividuation, the loss of a person's sense of individuality and personal responsibility. When reduced to "mob mentality," we are robbed of our sense of "self." We lose control of internal or moral constraints. We form lynch mobs and violent crowds.

We embark on genocide.

But we'll get to that momentarily.

The song begins as one door closes and another opens - this one, into a courtroom.

Welcome to "The Trial."

From the distance comes the sound of a bell; for whom does it toll? Thee, perhaps?

The oom-pah-pah of the tuba and the psychotic repetitive bleat of woodwinds (which do not echo any sort of sentiment of heroism), underscore a circus-like quality from the very beginning. The whole thing is very theatrical, reflecting a certain sense that Pink's world is a stage. These orchestral instruments are, in effect, the pit orchestra from the show that continues to be performed inside Pink's mind. They are voices, figments, that come from within Pink and represent his interpretations of what they would say, filtered through his own memories and emotions.

Presiding over this court is Pink's conscience. From a purely Christian standpoint, Pink has become the fallen man and now has to reconcile with his guilt. The act of being summoned to this courtroom is symbolic of a call to a higher spiritual existence.

If this was all there was to it, then Pink would be offered a typical Hollywood ending via some sort of redemption, ride off into the sunset and get his second chance. Rarely though, in the twisted-mirror universe of *The Wall,* does anything ever fall into the category of "typical."

Christian symbolism aside, far from being a work of religious nature, *The Wall* exists to reveal more about ourselves and what makes us tick.   Opening the proceedings is the Waters-voiced prosecutor who, like all the participants in the trial, is another character inside Pink's mind. Interesting though is how he addresses the judge as "Worm, your honor." Symbolic of decay (and to some extent in *The Wall,* death), the worm represents Pink's mortality. Eventually we will die, Waters is saying, and it will be the worms that render final judgment upon us as they eat our dead flesh.

The prisoner who now stands before you was caught red-handed showing feelings

Showing feelings of an almost human nature.

This will not do.

Notice how the word "feelings" is immediately followed by a wistful violin playing the same two note melody. Musically, this is done as a psychological echo, reinforcing the importance of the crime being about these particular feelings. It is also as an outright taunt.

Whereas Dictator Pink would likely face a war tribunal for crimes directly related to his *lack* of feelings and compassion, in this topsy-turvy world inside the twisted mirror, Pink is alternately accused of the crime of *being human*. Herein is the first real clue that we have not escaped dystopia; the Worm is revealed to also be a symbol of society's decay. This will be a trial before the same type of kangaroo court that hastily condemned Sartre's protagonist in his story, "The Wall." But that's not the only major existentialist literary reference at play here.

Published posthumously in 1926, a year after his death from starvation, Franz Kafka's novel, *The Trial* is about an everyman named Josef K who is arrested upon suspicion of acting in a way unlike how others are expected to act. He has committed no crime aside from the seemingly heinous act of just being an individual. A satire of the modern state, Josef K becomes thoroughly trapped in a totalitarian bureaucratic system. Eventually he is worn down and done in by this deplorable system, and more importantly, the erosion of his resistance to the machine. Also populated with very Dickensian characters that represent social commentary, Kafka's *The Trial* is a story about one man's inability to reach his own self amidst the maddening conflict of having to swim against the accepted social current.

In this case against Pink, the first witness called to testify as a character witness against him is the psychological embodiment of the Schoolmaster, who laments that all this "no good" could have been averted had he only been able to "flay" the boy into shape. "Flay," meaning the act of skinning a hide, seems to evoke the unflinching industrialized slaughterhouse. If that's the case, is it a *hide* that he wishes he could have skinned or a *Hyde*, as in Mr. Hyde, the dark and unsocial impulses lurking deep within.

On the surface it would seem that "no good" refers to the shenanigans perpetrated throughout Pink's life and the wake of destruction that followed. However, to some extent it concurrently refers directly to Roger and the creation of an allegorical work like *The Wall*, which shines a light upon the system's attempts to snuff out one's individuality like a cheap candle.

But my hands were tied,
The bleeding hearts and artists let him get away with murder.
Let me hammer him today.

This "murder" Waters has gotten away with pertains to the character assassination by *The Wall* of a system that refuses to capitulate or accept blame and still wants to place the individual on that assembly line and "hammer" him into a shape of their liking.

In his own defense, Pink pleads insanity.

...toys in the attic I am crazy,
Truly gone fishing.
They must have taken my marbles away.

Obviously these are all common and somewhat clichéd euphemisms that imply he's nuts. However, notice how there is an abdication of blame. It was *they* who took his marbles away. *They* stole from him. He is a victim. By inferring as much from the abdication of blame and the Greek chorus of the children's chorale that mockingly echoes Pink's words, we are able to believe this diagnosis was foisted upon him by a society wishing to categorize his non-standard behavior as abnormal.

All these authoritarian views of the characters we have heard in "The Trial" — the Schoolmaster, the Judge, the Prosecutor — take cues from the Super-Ego part of Pink's psyche. But that's about to change. Next to take the stand is Pink's libido: his Id.

Embodied by the figment of none other than his ex-wife.

You little shit you're in it now,

I hope they throw away the key.

You should have talked to me more often than you did, but no!

You had to go your own way.

Have you broken any homes up lately?

Just five minutes, Worm your honor,

Him and Me, alone.

Though her words may paint an unfavorable picture of Pink as a man, this interpretation of the wife's personality as filtered through Pink's mind is very unflattering at best. Openly hostile, passively aggressive, and possibly threatening violence, there is a sense here that despite the emotional suffering she endured while with him, inside of Mrs. Pink was some sort of dark persona all along. While Pink makes no allusion here that he is innocent of the infidelity for which he is accused, the appearance of a *Mrs. Hyde*-like violent being somewhat exonerates Pink (and to some extent, due to the autobiographical nature of *The Wall,* Roger) from being the only one to blame for the lack of communication.

Confronted with the hopelessness of his efforts to exist within society, the very idea that a schoolmaster would want to treat his students so inhumanely absolves Pink of behaving in the way the state wanted him to behave as a youth. By pleading insanity, he is distancing himself from being ultimately responsible for his actions. By implying he was victimized, Pink is telling us that nurture, not nature, led him to his predicament.

This leads us right to ground zero of his inability to connect with others.

His mother.

Immediately she refers to him as, "Baaaaabe!" Her eyes only see him as a helpless child. She heaps nothing but guilt upon him for his abandonment of her; she believes the cure for his ills is more (s)mothering. In her eyes, he is guilty of pushing her away for only showing the kind of natural affection a mother has for her baby.

Why'd he ever have to leave me?

Worm, your honor, let me take him home.

So is it any surprise that Pink finds himself to be a little bit nuts?

Crazy. Over the rainbow, I am crazy…

Hmmmm… Another possible *The Wizard of Oz* reference? Or is that just crazy?

Perhaps. Perhaps not.

There's very little doubt that the mental real estate owned by that particular phrase falls square on the movie version of Frank L. Baum's most famous literary work. One theory — floated around almost since *The Wizard of Oz* was first published — is that the book is actually a parable for Populism, the ideology that sides "the people" against "the elites." The Scarecrow was the American Farmer, simply lacking organization (a brain). The Tin Man was the Industrial Worker (Steel and Iron), The Lion, full of bluster, was the politician who lacks courage. In the book, Dorothy's slippers were silver not ruby red, representing the Silver Standard populists were fighting for; the Yellow Brick Road was the Gold Standard in use at the time. (The second book in the series, *The Marvelous Land of Oz*, is a blatant satire of the suffragette movement.) As such, it is more than just an anti-establishment fairy tale; it is something of a subversive document.

In the same way that Roger communicated with those conspiracy-minded "lookers" searching for the backmasking in his amusing message during "Empty Spaces," it is distinctly possible that this is his way to address the *Wizard of Oz/Dark Side of the Moon* mystery as being crazy talk.

On several occasions during *The Wall*, the midpoint of a song has consistently proven to be an important thematic milestone, whether through moments of musical or narrative transition. "The Trial" is no different. Here we have a telling lyric that, along with the very next line in the song, is set up to inform us of deeper layers buried deeper than a surface glance would expose.

There must have been a door there in the wall when I came in...

Waters is not saying there *is* a door in the wall, an easy escape. Instead he suggests that there is *no* way out. No exit.

In 1943 Jean-Paul Sartre published one of his most celebrated works of existentialist literature. A stage play, it portrayed a depiction of hell in which three very different people are punished by being locked in a room together for all eternity. There is no escape from this room and their difficulties dealing with each other drive them all mad. This play is the source of one of Sartre's best known quotes, "l'enfer, c'est les autres" which essentially translates into, "Hell is other people."

The name of this play?

No Exit.

Very much like Sartre's story "The Wall," his play *No Exit* deeply reflects his philosophical belief that every man is an autonomous individual who is determined by his own will alone. As such, it is his consequent separation from others that facilitates infallible liberty and free choice.

Whoa.

Do you still think that *The Wall* is just a story about a rock star who goes mad battling his demons and ends up becoming a fascist monster, only to be brought to justice and redeemed by being made to reveal his true self?

Pink doesn't find his redemption through the eyes of the court, however. These kangaroo proceedings allow for your honor, the Worm to not only pass judgment, but also to deliver the sentence without the trial to go to before a jury of Pink's peers. This, of course, is very similar to the "justice" served in Sartre's story "The Wall," after the protagonist is convicted and condemned by a hastily convened tribunal of enemy soldiers.

Even as judge Worm begins speaking, the musical sentiment is obvious. By re-introducing the same repeating Twilight Zone-esque distorted guitar lick featured during the dystopian moments of "Waiting For The Worms" (the same four notes that make up the melody to the chorus of "Another Brick In The Wall (Part 2)"), there is an implied sense of authoritarian conformity.

There is no way to see the judge as fair and unbiased. In fact, Gerald Scarfe's famous rendition of the judge, as seen in the movie version of *The Wall*, depicts the man as a talking asshole of sorts, which accounts for the sudden inclusion of a tuba in the musical arrangement to imply the figurative flatulence that would follow.

In all my years of judging I have never heard before
Of someone more deserving of the full penalty of law.

These are the published lyrics from "The Trial." Because Waters' vocal as the judge is doubled with an identical track pitched exactly one octave below the original, it's a bit hard to make the words out clearly, but listen closely and you will hear a distinct difference.

The word "law" sounds like it actually begins with a "w".

Waw?

Or is it an intentional lyrical misdirection meant to not only imply "penalty of law", but also "penalty of war?"

Though somewhat similar, the full penalty of war would include vanquishment, the abdication of power, and losing one's ability to determine their own fate.

Not to mention the possible loss of loved ones.

Is the judge implying that Pink/Roger deserved to have his father die in the war?

In the context of a Populist argument, such an inflammatory statement speaks to the idea of the elite classes sending the proletariat to fight their battles because that's what they deserve in exchange for the right to exist. Remember, the "court" isn't actually putting Pink on trial. The satirical nature of *The Wall* implies that it is Roger Waters putting *the motives of the system* up for closer inspection. The idea that Waters' father, originally a pacifist, was conned into enlisting for battle under a false sense of noble purpose, only to go to war and never return home is never too far away from the surface of the album's narrative.

By telling Pink he didn't deserve a father, the judge implies that the son is an embarrassment, particularly to this ideal of how a person should act within the bounds of so-called "civilized society." He is eliminating the possibility that the son could ever be his father's equal by saying he will never be the man his dad used to be.

The way you made them suffer,
Your exquisite wife and mother,
Fills me with the urge to defecate!

The wife and mother suffered because Pink, and perhaps to some extent, Roger, was not the person they expected and wanted him to be. He did not fit their mold of perfect son or husband.

In a nod to the satirical nature of the song and that the judge is a talking asshole, everything coming out of his mouth is all a load of shit and should be treated by the listener as such.

With the lecture from the bench now over, it is time for your honor, the Worm, to pass sentence.

Since, my friend, you have revealed your deepest fear
I sentence you to be exposed before your peers.
Tear down the wall!

This is not the Hollywood ending moment of rebirth, second chances and redemption. Whereas this may seem at first that Pink is to be freed from the mask that he wears, what he is getting in return is not liberation but instead assimilation. If the Schoolmaster's intention to expose Pink's weaknesses as a boy were bad, then how could this be any better?

His sentence is not justice in the moral sense. It is perverted justice meted out by a system that will do whatever it can to crush individuality. Much Josef K in Kafka's *The Trial*, Pink is being punished for being himself, an autonomous individual determined by his own will alone whose only crime was being true to his own personality, spirit, and character.

Just because I act differently, doesn't mean I'm insane. We are who we are. We are made up of our own experiences. Only by reconciliation of one's lighter and darker halves can a person become their true self.

Tear down the wall!
Tear down the wall!
Tear down the wall!

It is the mob that has come for Pink, to mete out the punishment prescribed by the state.

Tear down the wall!
Tear down the wall!
Tear down the wall!

It builds, growing into a frenzied discord, until, a growing rumble from the mob bursts into a massive explosion that sounds like a bomb unleashed on a target.

As the debris rains down, we are left only to ask, "What is left?"

*****

OUTSIDE THE WALL

The sun shines on a field the color of dark summer jade. From afar, they come — a small group of buskers, musical vagabonds really, playing their instruments as if they can summon a spirit from beyond an enormous wall that reaches unnaturally into the sky. Their tune is a pastoral incantation, challenging the unalienable forces of nature to allow them to take their comrade home.

From the dissipating rumble of the war-like explosions comes the wistful strain of a single clarinet. If this sounds at all familiar, it's because we return to the musical motif that began *The Wall* during those first seventeen seconds of "In the Flesh?"

All alone, or in twos,
The ones who really love you
Walk up and down outside the wall.

Lending them a certain feeling of incantation, the words are spoken, not sung. Here we stand before the ruins of Pink's wall in order to pay homage to the man. A group of children echo the lyrics, sounding like a chorus of angels and adding an element of purity to the message.

Some hand in hand
And some gathered together in bands.

The first line is a reference to family, the second to friends, especially as it pertains to Syd Barrett and how those in Pink Floyd still had love for their fallen comrade. When Waters mentions "bleeding hearts and artists," it is not only self-referential in terms of not being afraid to make a bold statement like *The Wall*, but a shout out to all of those who dare retain their individuality in the face of society's demands to assimilate.

And when they've given you their all, some stagger and fall,
After all it's not easy
Banging your heart against some mad bugger's wall.

So it would seem that Pink's metaphoric death, via the stripping away of his self-identity, was not in vain. That is demonstrated by these folks, who have traveled to the ruins of the wall in order to appreciate and celebrate individuality.

Those who really love you do so because of who you are inside. Society constantly tries to shape the individual into something of its own liking and isolates those who don't or won't comply. In the same way there is a certain loneliness to being unlike anyone else, there is a frustration to caring about the self-determined individual. Those who are willing to love you for who you are, despite your failings, are your true friends.

We build walls because of the Ego's need to reject rejection; we build walls because it gives us a sense of power, however limited, in situations where we have none.

In our interpersonal relationships with others who we truly are that is all that counts. Unfortunately, it is precisely here that we most often betray ourselves by trying to be what some other person expects us to be instead. The consequences of human responsibility — anguish over the decision, abandonment in making it alone, despair when it backfires — this, Sartre believed, is the character of human life.

It seems shocking that in 1931, Aldous Huxley's *Brave New World* decried a future in which technology destroys the basis of civilization by creating isolation and lack of civility. The obvious parallels between this sinister and prophetic warning and today's overindulgence and addiction to social media are hard to ignore.

Artists are informed by those who inspire them and the truths they hold in esteem. The best in their craft are often capable of taking very lofty themes and weaving them into allegories that allow people to gain illumination that they may have not been privy to previously. With *The Wall*, Waters has crafted a genius work that richly draws from masterpieces that preceded it. This is one of the most important albums of all time, if not *the* most important; it speaks to the human condition. It speaks about the relationships we have with each other. It speaks to our obligations to our dead relatives and ourselves. It asks us to question the institutions that we trust to shape us into people. It questions isolation.

It RESONATES within the human soul.

You have to wonder how much, if at all, Waters was influenced by another extremely popular double-length concept album, this one from the early 1970s:The Who's *Quadrophenia*. Even the title is a play on words to represent an exaggerated version of schizophrenia, as well as a nod to the then-hot audio fad of quadrophonic (4-speaker) sound. In *Quadrophenia*, the main character, Jimmy, feels isolation which causes paranoia. Ultimately, that leads to a self-destructive act that leaves Jimmy in true physical isolation — realizing too late that because of his choices, he's about to die.

You also have to wonder how much Waters was influenced by *La Traviata*, Giuseppe Verdi's mid-nineteenth century opera about isolation from love and how even amidst the company of gaudy friends, one can feel alone and helpless.

Though thematically similar, *The Wall* differs greatly from Sartre's "No Exit," because, unlike that damnable hell, there is indeed a door that leads out into the sunshine. Because we are allowed to see the grotesque qualities of the image shown to us in the twisted mirror, and understand them as perversions of who we are, from tragedy and downfall is birthed a triumph of the spirit and a redemption — not only of the soul, but of life itself.

Above all, Roger Waters is not just warning us to beware of repeating history's mistakes; he's begging us to understand the following:

Do not give into fear and intimidation.

Together we stand. Divided we fall.

And above all…

Stay true to yourself and you will never be anyone's slave.

Unlike utopian fiction, which often features an outsider that has the world shown to them, in *The Wall*, it is YOU who chooses to be an individual who is ultimately the hero of this story. Being a human being simply means you have the ability to create your own essence in the short time you are here on Earth. It is everyone's sole responsibility to give meaning to their own life by being as true to themselves as they can possibly be. It is also about accepting everyone, no matter their differences, because they are also capable of being individuals.

So it all ends, reflecting the universality of individual self-determination as well as the cyclical nature of life, repeating one's mistakes and the building and tearing down of walls, with Roger's voice asking, "Isn't this where…?"

This, in fact, is exactly where "We came in."

<<<<>>>>

ABOUT THE AUTHOR

MARK YOSHIMOTO NEMCOFF

Is an award-winning and bestselling author who has been featured on the hit TV show "Access Hollywood." Playboy Magazine praised Mark's comedy writing by saying, "Imagine Howard Stern dropping acid with Trey Parker and Jon Stewart while driving around downtown L.A. and you're almost there." Mark's writing has spread across a variety of media and television enterprises; he's written scripts directed by the likes of Bruce Campbell and he has written about music for top-end publications such as Blender Magazine. Mark also holds a degree in Music Production and Engineering from Boston's esteemed Berklee College of Music and after cutting his teeth working on albums by major label artists eventually became Vice President of the company responsible for the music on such hit sitcoms such as "That 70s Show" and "3rd Rock From the Sun." He is a successful composer in his own right, having scored original music on several network TV series, the 1994 Winter Olympics on CBS and major video game soundtracks. Mark was also one of the first creative visionaries to turn podcasting into a full time career after launching a comedy show recorded in his car. This turned into a stint on Sirius Satellite Radio five nights a week during drive time. From podcasting, Mark was cast as the co-host of a nationally-syndicated television show. On occasion, he has been known to moonlight as a voice-over artist and has been sought as a new media and branding consultant for Internet companies like GoDaddy and Verisign.

Mark currently resides in Los Angeles.

He can be reached at: MYN@WordSushi.com
Twitter.com/MYN
Facebook.com/MYNBooks

If you enjoyed this book, please tell your friends.

-MYN

ACKNOWLEDGEMENTS

Special thanks to R. Lee Brown whose editing and critical eye was really valuable in making this book what you see today. To Blake Morgan for helping me better understand how to attack the world as an indie creative without losing my soul and for the decades of friensdhip. Of course, big thanks to Mike Yusi for being my PCH podcast partner in crime and always pointing me in the right direction for great music. To my late parents, Barry and Keiko who took me to a laser rock show at the Philly Planetarium when I was a kid where I first heard "Run Like Hell" and was blown away by it. And of course to my awesome wife Marnie who rekindled my love of Pink Floyd and helped turn it into a complete obsession.

Plus, it goes without saying that I also want to send a big thanks to all of you out there who have followed and supported all of my books, shows and crazy exploits over the years. I promise there is much more where that came from.

ALSO BY MARK YOSHIMOTO NEMCOFF

NON-FICTION:
- Fatal Sunset: Deadly Vacations
- The Killing of Osama Bin Laden: How the Mission to Hunt Down a Terrorist Mastermind was Accomplished
- Where's My F*cking Latte? (And Other Stories About Being an Assistant in Hollywood)
- Go Forth and Kick Some Ass (Be the Hero of Your Own Life Story)
- Admit You Hate Yourself
- Pacific Coast Hellway Presents - Pissed Off: Is Better Than Being Pissed On
- Pacific Coast Hellway Presents: Porn Vs Chicken

FICTION:
- Diary of a Madman
- The Doomsday Club
- The Art of Surfacing
- Number One with a Bullet
- Shadow Falls: Badlands
- Shadow Falls: Angel of Death
- Killing My Boss
- Transistor Rodeo
- INFINITY

CPSIA information can be obtained at www.ICGtesting.com
Printed in the USA
LVOW11s1432010914

401879LV00001B/67/P